JOURNEY INTO A HOPE-FILLED LIFE

Seeds of Hope
from Ephesians
and Beyond

Clark Tatum

SUNSET

Sunset Institute Press
3710 34th Street ❖ Lubbock, Texas
806/788-3280/1 ❖ extschool@sibi.cc

Journey Into A Hope-Filled Life
Seeds of Hope From Ephesians and Beyond

Contents:

ACKNOWLEGEMENTS

This book is dedicated to

Virgil Yocham,

in appreciation for the spiritual encouragement,

guidance, and friendship he has shown me

since my earliest days of becoming a Christian.

A special "thank you" to

Sharon Tarbet

for her helpful proofreading

contribution to this book.

Introduction

This *Journey into a Hope-Filled Life* will nourish the hearts of those individuals who direct their attention to the only real source of hope – which is God and His Word. It is refreshing to know God desires we be a people overflowing with hope. Romans 15:13, *[13] May the God of hope fill you with all joy and peace as you trust in him, so that you may overflow with hope by the power of the Holy Spirit.* Most people would like to live with a little more hope. This book will take us on a journey over some prayerfully selected seeds of hope from the letter of Ephesians and beyond. We will draw upon Bible principles that will reinforce our hope in Christ.

When we slow down and survey the world around us, it appears we live in a world filled with hopelessness instead of hope. As Christians there is no reason for us to be short on hope. In fact, we are to spread an aroma of hope in the midst of the odor of hopelessness. There are good smells and bad smells. There are good smells like fresh homemade rolls out of the oven or the smell of a new car. Then there are bad smells like spoiled milk or rotten eggs.

When we lived in the Texas Panhandle, we could walk out our front door when the wind was blowing a certain direction and smell the foul odor from the nearby cattle feedlots. The smell was not inviting to us. I learned later it smelled much different to those who owned all those cattle. What smells good or bad has a lot to do with what we have been taught, or maybe more accurately what we have caught along the way. It is my prayer all Christians will resolve to be a people who overflow with the sweet fragrance of hope. Genuine hope is refreshing, inviting, and attractive.

In my book *Journey into a Fruit-Filled Life*, I was hopeful the readers would shower themselves in the entire list of the fruit of the Spirit found in Galatians 5:22-23. The fruit of the Spirit, like love, joy, and patience smells especially good in the common reality of a loveless, joyless, impatient world. God's way to live life is absolutely the best way. What is the result of living by the fruit of the Spirit? What is the result of living a hope-filled life? We are able to spread a beautiful aroma in our world wherever we are to the glory of the Lord Jesus Christ.

2 Corinthians 2:14-16, [14] *But thanks be to God, who always leads us in triumphal procession in Christ and through us spreads everywhere the fragrance of the knowledge of him.* [15] *For we are to God the aroma of Christ among those who are being saved and those who are perishing.* [16] *To the one we are the smell of death; to the other, the fragrance of life. And who is equal to such a task?* What a beautiful word picture – *the fragrance of life.*

There are two distinct smells we discharge as we live out our Christian lives in a non-Christian world. The location in which people find themselves in life's journey will determine the scent they give off when others are around them. To people who are tired of living hopeless lives we present a hope-filled pleasing aroma of life. We either will be the kind of person people enjoy being around or the kind of person people will try to avoid. They will either be curious and want to know more about the God who has infused our lives with His Spirit, or they will readily refuse to hear God's plan for abundant life. We may encounter some individuals who may not only refuse to hear more, they may even oppose God's very meaning of life.

Our hope based on God's love will be confusing for those who do not know anything about biblical hope or God's love. Hope and love commonly have a distorted definition in this world from biblical hope and love. As a result, while this contrast may be inviting to some people, to others it may be repulsive because they cannot believe such hope and love are possible. There will be people who simply do not understand God's kind of love or enduring eternal hope.

When we reflect a spirit of hope and love in times of trial, the people around us who do not know God will be confused as to how we could possibly have any kind of hope. It might be almost repulsive to them because they cannot fathom such endless hope or marvelous love. In such cases, we might do well to remember our own experience in accepting such hope and love when it was first introduced to us. Thankfully, for many of us there were a few Christians that did not give up on us. These believers graciously put up with the many barriers we attempted to place between ourselves and them. And over time we came to the realization that these people had something uniquely special and we wanted it too.

When we start asking around what life is all about, we readily receive a host of different answers. Many do ask such questions about life because they are without hope and realize in all their efforts to have hope, hope has alluded them. The answers we receive to our life's questions are only as good as where they originate. God designed life and He did it with great pleasure and eternal purpose. No less than seven times in Genesis 1 we find the phrase *"it was good."* And as God observed all He had made in Genesis 1:31, we can read He said, *"it was very good."*

God is good and we have the responsibility to direct people to what God says about abundant life and everlasting hope. Solomon, in Ecclesiastes, took on a research project like no other. He personally wanted to know where he could find meaning and purpose in life. He began his quest to find satisfaction in life and experimented with many things people do today. He used his wealth, education, and creative mind to find a meaningful, hope-filled life.

Solomon used a common phrase that he came back to again and again. He said, *"Utterly meaningless! Everything is meaningless"* (Ecclesiastes 1:2b). The word "meaningless" in the New International Version is found 32 times in Ecclesiastes. Other Bible translations like the English Standard Version and the New American Standard Bible uses the phrase, *"Vanity of vanities! All is vanity"* (Ecclesiastes 1:2). The words *"vanity"* or *"meaningless"* indicates no redeeming or lasting value.

It is hard to have hope when we come to the conclusion everything under the sun is empty, futile, and meaningless. Although, it is important to note that Solomon did not come to that conclusion at the end of his research experiment. He came to a much different conclusion by the end of Ecclesiastes. 12:13, *[13] Now all has been heard; here is the*

conclusion of the matter: Fear God and keep his command-
ments, for this is the whole [duty] of man.

Many believe today and perhaps we have thought this same
way in the past, "If only I could get that degree, or next degree
– then I'll be happy and satisfied!" Maybe we have said,
"When I get a better job, a bigger house, a nicer car, then I can
enjoy life and have hope in this hopeless world." Solomon
tried all these things and much more in his search for meaning
in life, but he came to the conclusion that we are to revere
and respect the Creator and stay with His plan for living life. It
is Solomon's conclusion that will bring us in our day to receive
the fragrance of life by following our Creator.

There is nothing sadder than a person living without hope.
Even some who claim to have hope today are void of the
hope we find in the New Testament. Hope in the New
Testament is connected to having a relationship with Jesus.
Genuine hope comes from knowing Jesus, obeying Jesus,
and by walking by faith with Him every day. The New
Testament teaches us we can have an abundance of hope
because God *leads us in triumphal procession in Christ.*
Therefore, the fragrance we obtain from the God of hope
signifies we have been blessed with eternal life.

I was not exactly sure where I would begin in Scripture to
write a book on hope. There were multiple verses that came
to the forefront of my mind. There are a number of places
in the Bible we could go to begin a journey on hope. It was
after much prayer and consideration, I decided to begin my
exploration on the subject of hope from God's letter to the
Christians in Ephesus.

The following journey through Ephesians and beyond will direct us to the source of real hope. We can find hope in living in God's pleasure. We can find hope in God's presence. We can find hope in God's praying people. We can find hope in God's power. We can find hope in God's precious love. We can find hope in God's provision. We can find hope in God's promise. We can find hope in God's purpose. We can find hope in God's plea for unity. We can find hope in God's plea for purity. We can find hope in God's prudence. We can find hope in God's plan. We can find hope in God's protection. May God bless our study into a hope-filled life.

FIND HOPE IN GOD'S PLEASURE
(Ephesians 1:1-10)

There are few words that resonate with more meaning or give more strength to us in life than the word hope. What a sharp contrast between the person who has hope and the person who has no hope. We will be exploring the idea of biblical hope through this book as we direct our attention to "The Book." It is in the book we call the Bible where we find the foundation for solid hope.

Christian hope comes from being in Christ and learning about what He has accomplished for people of faith. The idea of hope is often misunderstood. Christian hope is distinctly different from the concept of hope held by the majority of people. Many people claim to have hope, but their hope eludes them in life's storms. Why does hope seem so fleeting in our world? It is because people do not have biblical hope.

The world's hope is a wishful hope. Christian hope is confident expectant hope. The Christian's hope comes from believing what God has said in His Word is one hundred percent true. Wishful hope is the hope of wishing for something to happen, but lacking any confidence that it will for sure happen. The world's hope is flimsy and readily escapes us when things do not go as we hope they will.

A person may say, "I hope it rains today," or "I hope it does not rain today." In either case, we are not absolutely sure it will rain or be a dry day. Although, I must admit we could be a bit surer if we lived in Phoenix, Arizona or in Mobile, Alabama as to whether or not it was going to be a rainy or sunshiny day. The city of Phoenix only receives an average of 9 inches of rainfall a year while the city of Mobile receives an average of 69 inches. The point here concerning hope is that our world commonly uses the word hope in an unsure way. This kind of hope lacks one hundred percent confidence.

It is not that people in general do not have hope at all in this world, but rather their hope lacks one hundred percent certainty. I am sure we have all said things like: "I hope I get this job" or "I hope I will be accepted to the university" or "I hope I can qualify for the loan," or "I hope I don't run out of gas" or "I hope I don't catch the flu." We have all hoped for things along this line. There is nothing at all sinful about this type of hope, but it is not biblical hope.

Even the world's view of hope can be helpful at times. When we started high school we likely would not have done so well as freshmen if we did not embrace the wishful hope of one day becoming graduating seniors. Teenagers live with a wishful hope of one day being on their own and leaving their parents' house. There is nothing wrong with having this kind of hope. In fact, loving parents have a similar hope for their own children. We should value independence. Only let us be cautious in our understanding of healthy independence. We should not allow our spirit of independence to hinder our dependence upon God.

We all need a measure of hope, but there is a sharp contrast between the wishful hope and biblical hope. Unless we move beyond the simple wishful hope to the deeper understanding of the godly hope, we will find ourselves living hopeless lives instead of hope-filled lives. This will be especially true when we meet life's more difficult situations or circumstances. When we experience heartache and tragedy without genuine hope, we will more likely have to deal with doubt, disillusionment, and possibly dangerous discouragement.

When we embrace biblical hope, we discover the strength to productively press on through the tears of life's troubles. Our world does not lack wishful hope, it lacks biblical hope. Biblical hope can refresh our souls and comfort our hearts. This is the kind of hope we need and can live with daily in this hopeless world. The seeds of hope we can discover from Ephesians will help us be able to endure our most pressing problems without losing hope.

Biblical hope ushers into our hearts a total confidence in the goodness of God even in what may seem like a hopeless situation. Biblical hope brings comfort and provides support because our hope has foundation in God's Word. Biblical hope is rooted in faith and is always going to be attached to God's Word. This is the hope we can have as an anchor during the storms we face in this life.

The Christians in the city of Ephesus believed that Jesus not only spoke truth, He was truth. Ephesians 4:21, *²¹ Surely you heard of him and were taught in him in accordance with the truth that is in Jesus*. When our hearts are troubled and we are feeling the weight of the world on our backs, we must set our hearts on God's truth. We must begin with the truth of Scripture to come to know true hope. Enduring hope comes from saturating our minds on the wonderful truths we find in the Word. The letter of Ephesians is filled with truth that will keep us from complaining about what happens or does not happen to us in life. We will dig deeper into these truths in our journey of hope.

Jesus and His Word represent an anchor for a believer's hope. *We have this hope as an anchor for the soul, firm and secure* (Hebrews 6:19a). If we will wrap our arms of faith around God's truth, Satan will never be successful in stealing our hope when we encounter trials. When I mention we live in a hopeless world I am speaking of a world that does not hold to God's definition of hope. Hebrews 11:1, *[1] Now faith is being sure of what we hope for and certain of what we do not see.* The wording in the King James Version is insightful. The Bible reads, *[1] Now faith is the substance of things hoped for, the evidence of things not seen* (Hebrews 11:1).

Faith has "substance" and that substance links itself to hope. The Bible translations point to the stability of hope that comes by faith. Hope is based on securely holding firmly to the promises of God founded in the Word of God. The New International Version reads; *Let us hold unswervingly to the hope we profess, for he who promised is faithful* (Hebrews 10:23). This shows us the connection between faith and hope. The New American Standard Bible and the King James Version uses the phrase *"hold fast"* in Hebrews 10:23 instead of the phrase *"hold unswervingly."*

We can have an unwavering measure of hope in the loneliest, darkest, even the strangest of places when we catch a glimpse of God's good pleasure. Ephesians 1:1-10, *[1] Paul, an apostle of Christ Jesus by the will of God, To the saints in Ephesus, the faithful in Christ Jesus: [2] Grace and peace to you from God our Father and the Lord Jesus Christ. [3] Praise be to the God and Father of our Lord Jesus Christ, who has blessed us in the heavenly realms with every spiritual blessing in Christ. [4] For he chose us in him before the creation of the world to be holy and blameless in his sight. In love [5] he predestined us to be adopted as his sons through Jesus Christ, in accordance with his pleasure and will – [6] to the praise of his glorious grace, which he has freely given us in the One he loves. [7] In him we have redemption through his blood, the forgiveness of sins, in accordance with the riches of God's grace [8] that he lavished on us with all wisdom and understanding. [9] And he made known to us the mystery of his will according to his good pleasure, which he purposed in Christ, [10] to be put into effect when the times will have reached their fulfillment – to bring all things in heaven and on earth together under one head, even Christ.*

Do not read lightly over the word's *"pleasure"* (v.5) or *"good pleasure"* (v.9). Both the King James Version and the New King James Version insert the phrase *"good pleasure"* twice (Ephesians 1:5,9). There is a vital connection between the Bible concept of faith and God's good pleasure. God's blessing us with spiritual blessings lifts our spirits with hope in what otherwise would be an absolutely hopeless situation.

What is the hope we can attain by learning what it is that makes up God's good pleasure? What is God's good pleasure? It is God's good pleasure to bless His people with every spiritual blessing. Wow! Ephesians 1:3, *³ Praise be to the God and Father of our Lord Jesus Christ, who has blessed us in the heavenly realms with every spiritual blessing in Christ.*

God's good pleasure is to bless, and bless, and bless us some more in the heavenly realms in Christ. Since the letter of Ephesians was written to Christians, we can know God wanted His people to better understand His pleasure and unending desire to bless His people. God has worked and continues to work even now to fill our hearts with hope. There are signs of hopelessness all around us that remind us the devil is also working. The devil works to keep people from having hope.

If we will listen, learn, and apply what God tells us in Ephesians, we will never have to concern ourselves with the devil robbing us of our hope in Christ. God wants us to have a hope in this life that has weight and value not only for this life, but life in heaven. The Apostle Paul speaks of this type of hope to Christians who have had to say goodbye to their loved ones for the last time on this side of heaven. 1 Thessalonians 4:13-14, *¹³ Brothers, we do not want you to be ignorant about those who fall asleep, or to grieve like the rest of men, who have no hope. ¹⁴ We believe that Jesus died and rose again and so we believe that God will bring with Jesus those who have fallen asleep in him.*

The apostle penned these words by way of the Holy Spirit to clear up some confusion about those who have *"fallen asleep."* The word "asleep" is used three times in 1

Thessalonians chapter 4. Each time the word "asleep" is used it references those believers who have died with their belief and hope firmly rooted in Jesus. Does biblical hope make a difference in the way we view death? Absolutely!

No matter where we live, the funeral home business is always busy. As a preaching minister I have conducted my share of memorial services for grieving families. I have directed two separate memorials on the same day more than once for families who have lost loved ones. And once I officiated three memorials on the same day. We can know by our experience and observation the difference everlasting hope can make during times of grief. By observing people at memorial services, we are able to recognize those who believe in God and have some measure of faith.

When a believer faces the reality of the death of a loved one, he will grieve, but not as those who have no hope. When death invades our families, we grieve and it is natural to grieve. We may express our grief differently, but everyone grieves. Believers and unbelievers grieve. Any funeral director will acknowledge that there is a distinct difference between faith-families and non-faith families in the grieving process. Faith families are hope-filled families.

Being receivers of God's good pleasure gives us countless reasons to have hope no matter what happens on this side of heaven. Hope gives us the foundation to grieve differently than those without faith. It is worth repeating this truth. 1 Thessalonians 4:13, [13] *Brothers, we do not want you to be ignorant about those who fall asleep, or to grieve like the rest of men, who have no hope.*

The term "fall asleep" is a wonderful way to speak of a believer's death. In John chapter 11 Jesus learned that His friend Lazarus from Bethany was sick. Two days later He told His disciples they needed to return to the area of Judea. His closest followers frowned on that idea because some Jews from that area had recently tried to stone Jesus. Bethany was only two miles from Jerusalem where the deep-seated hatred and animosity towards Jesus was most intense. Nonetheless, Jesus told them, *[11b] "Our friend Lazarus has fallen asleep; but I am going there to wake him up"* (John 11:11b).

When Jesus arrived in Bethany, Lazarus had already died and had been dead for several days. Martha and Mary were naturally grieving over their brother's death. Jesus loving them spoke comforting words to these sisters. He shared with Martha some of the most hope-filled words anyone could ever hear at the death of their loved one. John 11:23-25, *[23] Jesus said to her, "Your brother will rise again." [24] Martha answered, "I know he will rise again in the resurrection at the last day." [25] Jesus said to her, "I am the resurrection and the life. He who believes in me will live, even though he dies."*

Jesus spoke reassuring and soothing words that had to inject hope into Martha's heart. Jesus was telling Martha in John 11 that His faithful followers will not experience any separation from God. This truth was reinforced later as one of the great blessings of the Christian faith. Romans 8:38-39, *[38] For I am convinced that neither death nor life, neither angels nor demons, neither the present nor the future, nor any powers, [39] neither height nor depth, nor anything else in all creation, will be able to separate us from the love of God that is in Christ Jesus our Lord.*

Jesus did much more for Martha and Mary that day than simply speak words of hope. He went on to raise Lazarus to life after being dead for four days. We can praise God for the reality that darkness, sin, and death does not have the last word. It was God's good pleasure to bless us in the heavenly realms and this incredible truth helps us to live hope-filled lives.

I have noticed most people understand that one day they will die. But I have also noticed while they understand that reality, few people expect it to be the day they die. We all realize there are things that happen in life we cannot see coming until they arrive at our doorstep. These unexpected tragedies can be heart wrenchingly difficult. There are things we cannot envision happening or ever anticipate happening, even down deep we know they could happen.

Hope connected to truth provides believers the ability to have the assurance that what God says in His Word is true. That can be most comforting in times of loss. Since we do not know the exact day we will die or how we will die, we must make our spiritual preparations for death today. For example, I do not know with any certainty I will finish writing this book, or for that matter this first chapter. However, I am not being pessimistic as I sit in this comfortable chair typing away.

I am not being pessimistic when I mention the brevity of life, I am just being realistic. I have conducted funeral services for families whose loved one died while they were sitting in a chair. We do not know how we will die. And I have no plans to die before completing this book. However, when we take an honest view of life as God designed it, we understand God did not create any of us to live on this earth forever. There will be a day all of us will not complete a book, we will not finish writing, and plans will go unfulfilled. Although, we can take heart in knowing God created us to live forever.

The blessing of our one day living forever with God must begin in our walking with God now prior to falling asleep in Jesus. We have no second chances to go God's way after death. We may not have a two-minute warning when death strikes like we have in football. The last day for some people on earth will be unexpected, so we need to prepare spiritually the best we can for both the expected things in life and the unexpected things. We may not know the day of our death or the way of our death, but we can know as a result of God's good pleasure the blessing of living hope-filled lives. We can never lose when Jesus writes the end of our story.

This is where God's good pleasure and will resurfaces in our reading of Ephesians. We can be confident as a result of God's good pleasure and our faith in God that we when we close our eyes in Jesus, we will continue to enjoy our spiritual blessings in Christ. Being in Christ and remaining faithful to the Lord is what gives us confidence that we are prepared to die on any given day.

It is always going to be helpful for us to remember there is only one safe day and one safe place to die and that is in

Christ Jesus. Why? Because God in His good pleasure has blessed us beyond measure in Christ. In Ephesians 1:3-10 we learn it was the pleasure of God to provide numerous blessings. It was the pleasure of God to choose us as His creative masterpiece and adopted us as His sons.

God chose us according to chapter 1:4 and the idea is repeated in verse 11. God chose us. What an amazing statement and we will consider what God choosing us means in some detail. But first let us just think about how we feel when we are chosen for something special. Maybe all these years later we recall the feeling we had when our name was called to be a player on that sports team. Perhaps we can remember being chosen for a part in the school play or being chosen as a representative of our school for some regional or state competition.

We may know the feeling that comes with being chosen to be a player on the all-star team or to compete in a marching band competition. We all remember applying for a certain job we really wanted, and then being chosen for the job. There is nothing like the feeling of being chosen. The feeling of being chosen in such a way does not quickly leave us.

There is another feeling that we all have experienced and it is a much different emotion. We all know the feeling that we get when we are not chosen for the team or the job, and that is what makes being chosen so special. There is an old story that has circulated through the years about a preacher that was chosen to speak for a certain charitable organization. When he was asked to speak, he immediately expressed his delight in having the opportunity.

After the event was over, the program chairman who had asked him to speak handed the preacher a check. The preacher said with some embarrassment, "Oh, I could not possibly accept this check. I just appreciate the honor of being asked to speak. You must have better uses for your money – just apply it to one of those needs." The chairman asked him, "Well would you mind if we put this amount into our special fund?" The preacher replied, "Of course not, but what is the special fund for?" The chairman said, "It is so we can get a better speaker next year." The preacher was chosen, but if the organization had to do over again, they would choose someone else.

God chose us out of His pleasure and God did not make a mistake when He chose us. He did not choose us because we were talented, educated, or a gifted speaker. He chose us out of His good pleasure and that truth is worth repeating over and over. That fact gives us hope. As difficult as it is for us to accept, we are worth the entire world to God. The crucifixion of Jesus proves this point.

Ephesians 1:4, *⁴ For he chose us in him before the creation of the world to be holy and blameless in his sight.* If God had to do it over again, He would choose us again. That is a hard concept for us to get our arms around because of our shortcomings and sins. What will help us as we continue through Ephesians is to remember we are getting God's view of our value, not our view. We were chosen not because we are good, but because God is good and He values us.

By God's pleasure He chose us and freed us from our sin. He called us to follow His Son and our Savior. He chooses to be patient with us while He shapes us to His glory. There is a hope that comes from being chosen by God and being adopted as one of His sons. May we take hold of the hope available to us solely based on our Christian identity and being chosen to be a member on God's team. Yes, there is nothing like being chosen and being placed in the body of Christ.

It was the pleasure and will of God which granted us grace and redemption through the blood of Christ. We can find hope in the glory of God's grace (Ephesians 1:6). We can find hope in the riches of God's grace (Ephesians 1:7). God lavishes grace on those "in Christ." As we journey through Ephesians, I will call our attention to the word grace nearly every time it appears because it is closely connected to our living hope-filled lives.

We can learn from what was written that it brings God great pleasure to fill us with our most desperate need – His glorious grace. The Apostle Paul in Romans 15:4 gives inspired confidence of the truth found in the Old Testament Scripture. Romans 15:4, *4 For everything that was written in the past was written to teach us, so that through endurance and the encouragement of the Scriptures we might have hope.* We can learn from what was written in both the Old and New Testaments that it brought pleasure to God to make our redemption possible.

The New Testament writers occasionally reference Old Testament writings that foreshadow Jesus or His sufferings. For instance, Isaiah 53:4-6, *4 ... he took up our infirmities and carried our sorrows, yet we considered him stricken by God, smitten by him, and afflicted. [5] But he was pierced for our transgressions, he was crushed for our iniquities; the punishment that brought us peace was upon him, and by his wounds we are healed. [6] We all, like sheep, have gone astray, each of us has turned to his own way; and the LORD has laid on him the iniquity of us all.*

We cannot begin to imagine how difficult it had to be for God the Father to send His beloved Son to this earth to become a sacrifice for our sins. What we can do is read in the Bible how Jesus left the glories of heaven to robe Himself in the flesh so He could become our sacrificial lamb. His coming to seek and save the lost was in complete harmony with God's pleasure. From the beginning God predetermined we could be on God's team.

Ephesians 1:5 [5] *having predestined us to adoption as sons by Jesus Christ to Himself, according to the good pleasure of His will* (New King James Version). The word "predestined" here in simplest terms implies God marked out beforehand how that adoption process would take place. We should not get bogged down on that word "predestined" as if we never had a choice in the matter. We do have a choice and if we are Christians, we made the right choice.

Acts 2:21 reads, [21] *...everyone who calls on the name of the Lord will be saved.* The calling on the Lord God is a choice we make that necessitates our believing, confessing, repenting, and being baptized into Christ. Ananias was sent by God to share a message with Saul. Saul was his Jewish name, but Saul will become more commonly known in Scripture by his Roman name Paul.

In Acts 22 Ananias spoke God's message to Saul. Acts 22 with Acts 22:14-16, [14] *Then he said: 'The God of our fathers has chosen you to know his will and to see the Righteous One and to hear words from his mouth.* [15] *You will be his witness to all men of what you have seen and heard.* [16] *And now what are you waiting for? Get up, be baptized and wash your sins away, calling on his name.'* Verse 16 gives us inspired insight as to what it means to call upon the name of the Lord.

Paul had a choice, as we do, when it came to responding to Jesus. We should remember Ephesians was written to people who had already become Christians. Therefore, we should notice the emphasis the inspired writer Paul (chosen by God to be an apostle) put on a person being "in Christ." Being in Christ is the specific location where we can receive every spiritual blessing. Therefore, being in Christ is an important matter.

We need to be in Christ to have access to the blessings of God's pleasure through Christ. The words "redemption" and "forgiveness" and "grace" have everything to do with who we are in Christ. The term "in Christ" or "in Him" is significant because it is only there that we can obtain the stream of spiritual blessings. People who love God and have godly sorrow over their sins will readily express a willingness to confess Jesus as Lord and call upon the Lord by being baptized into Christ.

Galatians 3:26-27, [26] *You are all sons of God through faith in Christ Jesus,* [27] *for all of you who were baptized into Christ have clothed yourselves with Christ.* Faith in Christ puts us in touch with all the spiritual blessings available in Christ. When people put on Christ in baptism, they become beneficiaries of spiritual blessings in harmony with God's pleasure and will. Colossians 2:12, *12 having been buried with him in baptism and raised with him through your faith in the power of God, who raised him from the dead.*

After we call upon the Lord the way Saul did in Acts 22:16, we can enjoy eternal hope. We need eternal hope in the future and we need eternal hope in the present. Christians must remember that when we were in desperate need to find hope in a hopeless world, God made hope available to us. When we were in desperate need for hope it pleased God to make a way we could be released from the condemnation of our sins through the blood of Jesus.

Ephesians 1:7, *7 In him we have redemption through his blood, the forgiveness of sins, in accordance with the riches of God's grace.* Is it any wonder that the apostle – knowing the many hope-based truths he would be revealing to God's faithful – would begin the letter of Ephesians with praise for God? Ephesians 1:3, *3 Praise be to the God and Father of our Lord Jesus Christ, who has blessed us in the heavenly realms with every spiritual blessing in Christ.*

Hope that stems from faith produces a confident expectation that those in Christ are recipients of His spiritual blessings. God's breath of hope and the fingerprints of hope can be felt on every word in the Ephesian letter. Hope allows us the strength to live life to the fullest.

CHAPTER 1 – QUESTIONS
TO DISCUSS, DEVELOP, AND DETERMINE

1. Where does Christian hope originate? What must we begin with to come to know true hope?

2. How is Christian hope different from the concept that people generally have concerning hope today? Why does hope seem so fleeting to so many people in the world?

3. Describe the hope we can gain and attain by learning more about what it is that brings pleasure to God. What does the apostle express praise to God for in Ephesians 1:3?

4. What does the term "asleep" or "fall asleep" mean in 1 Thessalonians 4:13? What blessing from God can we hold onto during these lonely times? How does this blessing reinforce our hope?

5. Where according to the Bible does a person need to be in order to be a recipient of every spiritual blessing provided by Christ?

6. What are some specific blessings Christians enjoy as a result of God's good pleasure in Ephesians 1:1-10?

7. Describe the blessing of being chosen by God and how we can find hope in this Bible truth. Explain how God's choosing us still leaves us with a choice to make.

8. Where does God always leads His people? (See the Introduction Section)

FIND HOPE IN GOD'S PRESENCE
(Ephesians 1:7, 11-14)

When I was a young boy, I remember my parents had a television set in the living room. Saturday morning cartoons were a special treat for me since I was not allowed to watch television during the week. I thought it was great to have a television set because even at my young age I realized not every family had a television. As I think back on those Saturday mornings there was a distinct contrast between televisions in that day and the televisions children watch their cartoons on today.

When I was a child our television was not impressive at all in comparison to today's models. The television picture was black-and-white and it was one big television. I am not talking about a big screen television either. In fact, the screen was not all that big. The television screen was positioned in the center of a large wooden cabinet that had legs. In those days many televisions were placed in a cabinet and was referred to as a television console.

My memory tells me our television set was one of our nicest pieces of furniture. While the cabinet the television was in looked nice, the reception on the screen was not sharp or clear. In those days people regularly used rabbit ear antennas which sat right on top of the television. I recall my mother putting aluminum foil around the two rabbit ear antennas which she said would improve our reception. I watched my share of grainy black and white images.

There were no remote controls in that day. No, we had to actually get up and down to turn on and off the television. We had to press a small button located near the channel dial and be patient for the picture to appear. After we turned it on, we had to wait for the television to warm up, because when we pushed or maybe pulled the button to turn it on, nothing seemed to happen for a while.

Some of us can remember those days when our televisions needed time to warm up, while others cannot relate to that kind of experience at all. We may remember waiting for the picture to appear on the screen which is a foreign idea to people today. We would turn the set on and then hope we would see a small dot appear in the middle of the screen. If we saw the dot, we knew it would probably work and things were going to be OK. After a few seconds the dot would become a line that stretched from one side of the screen to the other and then suddenly, the line would explode into a bright square that would become a clear picture.

I mentioned my television experience to say that when we open the letter of Ephesians in search of seeds of hope, we do not have to wait at all. The seeds of hope start showing up on the screen of our minds as instantly as we might turn on our color television set today. The first few verses of Ephesians that we have already considered do not give us a dot on the screen or a period of time where we have to wait to get a beautiful picture.

The picture the apostle paints for us in the first few verses of Ephesians instantly begins to fill us with hope. Yet it is only a dot of the rich blessings we will continue to discover in Ephesians and beyond. If for any reason our reception was a little blurry due to the massive selection of abundant blessings Paul has recorded for us already, like being chosen by God, adopted as His sons, or receiving the forgiveness of sins, we have opportunity to finetune our spiritual antennas. The picture of the spiritual blessings we have in Christ will become even more clear. It will be as if we were reading or hearing these scriptures on the Imax picture screen of our minds.

We can have hope in God's presence and live in His presence based on what the apostle has already written in Ephesians without exploring new ground. Therefore, before we progress any further in our journey into this hope-filled letter, let me expand our picture screen of the redemption blessing we looked at in the previous chapter. Ephesians 1:7, *7 In him we have redemption through his blood, the forgiveness of sins, in accordance with the riches of God's grace.* The word "redemption" comes from the word that literally means, "to release from captivity."

In the New Testament world, "redemption" was tied to the idea of paying a ransom. The Greek word for "redemption" (APOLUTROSIS) in Ephesians is made up of a compound word. The word indicates a release by way of a payment. Like the slaves in the Roman Empire, if we were going to be set free from sin's slavery, a ransom had to be paid. However, in our case no amount of money could set us free. All the money in the world would not be enough to release us from our sins.

There was only one way to bring us back into a relationship with God and the blessing of living in the presence of God. 1

Peter 1:18-19, *¹⁸ For you know that it was not with perishable things such as silver or gold that you were redeemed from the empty way of life handed down to you from your forefathers, ¹⁹ but with the precious blood of Christ, a lamb without blemish or defect.* Jesus was the lamb without blemish through which flows His blood that brings forgiveness.

We have redemption and the forgiveness of sins through Jesus' blood. The Greek word (APHESIS) for "forgiveness" denotes a release from bondage. The word basically carries the idea "to send away, to depart, to release, to cancel." God at the high cost of His only begotten Son sends our sins away so they no longer stand between us and a Holy God. This is the only reason we can abide in God's presence.

The Levitical sacrificial system under the Old Testament was extremely detailed in the process of offering sacrifices for sin. Day-by-day people offered sacrifices but they would not catch their own sin every single day, even if they wanted to, so God made a provision – called the Day of Atonement. The sacrifices on the Day of Atonement in the Old Testament prefigured Jesus' sinless once for all sacrifice that sets us free from the condemnation of sin.

Once a year under the Old Covenant God brought the entire nation into a process known as Day of Atonement meaning "a day of covering." The Day of Atonement would be an annual reminder of their sins. It was an extraordinarily special day and a day that was mixed with fear and, toward the end of the day, a celebration if all went well. The Day of Atonement was the only day of the year where all Jews were commanded to fast. All across the nation on that day they would go without food.

As the people looked out across the nation, they would see some people wearing old sackcloth as a sign of repentance. Other people would have ashes sprinkled on their head showing their sorrow of sin. On this day the entire nation of Israel felt the weight of their sin.

The high priest would offer many sacrifices on this day but the highlight of the day was when the High Priest would take two unblemished goats according to Leviticus the 16th chapter. The Israelite community on this day would bring two male goats as a sin offering and a ram for a burnt offering. All of Israel would be silent and subdued hoping and praying God would accept the high priest and the sacrifice for their sins.

The high priest would take that goat that was to be a sin offering, slaughter it, and take the blood and carry the blood through the veil in the tabernacle that separated the Holy Place from the Most Holy Place. He would then present the blood as an offering for the sins of Israel. After the priest would slay one of the goats, he would then bring the live goat before the people and lay both of his hands on the head of the goat and begin to confess the sins of Israel.

This priestly act of sacrifice, coupled with the confession, symbolized that the live goat was taking on the sins of the people. This demonstrated to the people of Israel that God was transferring the guilt of the people to the goat. After the high priest completed the confession process, the goat called the "scapegoat" would be led out into the desert and turned loose (Leviticus 16:20-26). As the people watched the escape goat being led away into the desert, they were visibly aware that goat is carrying away their sins.

God's acceptance of the sacrifice of the high priest on this day meant they would have a fresh start with God. The living goat became a visual reminder of their sins (Hebrews 10:1-4). All the blood sacrifices in the Old Testament were symbolic of this sin sending away process. We have all heard the expression, "he became a scapegoat." The idea comes from Leviticus. Jesus became the ultimate scapegoat to redeem us.

Hebrews 9:12-15, *[12] He did not enter by means of the blood of goats and calves; but he entered the Most Holy Place once for all by his own blood, having obtained eternal redemption. [13] The blood of goats and bulls and the ashes of a heifer sprinkled on those who are ceremonially unclean sanctify them so that they are outwardly clean. [14] How much more, then, will the blood of Christ, who through the eternal Spirit offered himself unblemished to God, cleanse our consciences from acts that lead to death, so that we may serve the living God! [15] For this reason Christ is the mediator of a new covenant, that those who are called may receive the promised eternal inheritance – now that he has died as a ransom to set them free from the sins committed under the first covenant.*

Jesus was the only one who could satisfy a Holy God for penalty of our sins. 2 Corinthians 5:21, *[21] God made him who had no sin to be sin for us, so that in him we might become the righteousness of God.* We can live in the presence of God because we have been made right with God by way of redemption. What an exhilarating truth! The sinless blood of Christ that poured down from the cross made it possible for the chain to be broken that separated us from God and robbed us of hope. What a picture we get on the screen of our minds when we see the words *"we have redemption through His blood"* (Ephesians 1:7).

Hebrews 9:27-28, *[27] Just as man is destined to die once, and after that to face judgment, [28] so Christ was sacrificed once to take away the sins of many people; and he will appear a second time, not to bear sin, but to bring salvation to those who are waiting for him.* Three truths we can take from this passage. 1. Death is a certainty. 2. Final judgment is a reality. 3. Eternal salvation can be ours. The blood of Jesus may not take away every sinful pain, but we can know the blood of Jesus can erase the penalty of our sin.

Today we are told that under the New Covenant Jesus offered the one perfect sacrifice for every person. Hebrews 10:12-14, *[12] But when this priest had offered for all time one sacrifice for sins, he sat down at the right hand of God. [13] Since that time he waits for his enemies to be made his footstool, [14] because by one sacrifice he has made perfect forever those who are being made holy.* Jesus became our Passover Lamb so we might be forgiven and be in God's presence.

Our next passage from Ephesians along with a few other verses in the Bible will highlight the hope that derives from living in God's presence. Ephesians 1:11-14, *[11] In him we were also chosen, having been predestined according to the plan of him who works out everything in conformity with the purpose of his will, [12] in order that we, who were the first to hope in Christ, might be for the praise of his glory. [13] And you also were included in Christ when you heard the word of truth, the gospel of your salvation. Having believed, you were marked in him with a seal, the promised Holy Spirit, [14] who is a deposit guaranteeing our inheritance until the redemption of those who are God's possession – to the praise of his glory.*

We have numerous reasons to have hope from these four verses alone. We can celebrate and praise God for Bible truths like the fact God is working out everything according to His plan. God's plans are perfect and He works out His plan according to His purpose. Ephesians 1:11 is not the only place we find the word "purpose" in the letter. We will spend some time on God's purpose when we get to chapter three, but I will mention a few things here in light of verse 11.

We are told once again in Scripture that God works. It is no surprise to us, and it is certainly no surprise He works for our good. God is good and we can enjoy redemption because God set a plan in motion that was designed entirely for our good. God is good and will always be good. Out of His goodness when we were not doing right, GOD perfectly worked His plan. His plan was so flawless that it would allow redeemed sinners to have uninterrupted fellowship with God.

1 John 1:1-3, *[1] That which was from the beginning, which we have heard, which we have seen with our eyes, which we*

have looked at and our hands have touched – this we proclaim concerning the Word of life. [2] The life appeared; we have seen it and testify to it, and we proclaim to you the eternal life, which was with the Father and has appeared to us. [3] We proclaim to you what we have seen and heard, so that you also may have fellowship with us. And our fellowship is with the Father and with his Son, Jesus Christ.

The message of 1 John is all about life and fellowship with God, not merely existence. The words "that which" was from the beginning was uninterrupted fellowship. That is exactly what God had with His creation in the beginning. Yes, I understand Jesus was in the beginning (John 1:1-3). Jesus was involved in the creation account of Genesis, and Genesis means beginning. But I believe in 1 John the apostle is emphasizing not only Jesus but the life as represented by the one who said He was the Life (John 14:6).

John in his introductory remarks wanted to state clearly the blessing of having fellowship with God. It is worth considering that in the beginning what was so precious to Adam and Eve in the Garden was the quality of life they enjoyed with God. The life represented uninterrupted fellowship. This couple had a walking talking relationship with God. John made a point he had seen the life that was in the beginning. This fellowship means we can live in God's presence.

John does not want us to miss this life. He emphasizes he is not passing on a rumor that has been passed down through the ages. John himself had experienced life – uninterrupted fellowship with God. And this life had so captivated him it awakened all of his senses. This fellowship with God was proclaimed to him and he heard it and as an apostle he was passing it on according to God's plan. John had seen this life in Jesus that he never knew existed prior to knowing about it from the Word of Life.

How did we feel when we first heard about the possibility of uninterrupted fellowship with God? Perhaps we felt similar to John in the sense when we heard about eternal life, we could not shake it from our thoughts. In our own way we looked at life, gazed at the idea and it captured our attention. John goes on to tell us his hands touched this life and now proclaim the message of fellowship from Jesus who we have experienced life.

We who are enjoying redemption today can have the hope of God's presence today. 1 John 1:5-7, *⁵ This is the message we have heard from him and declare to you: God is light; in him there is no darkness at all. ⁶ If we claim to have fellowship with him yet walk in the darkness, we lie and do not live by the truth. ⁷ But if we walk in the light, as he is in the light, we have fellowship with one another, and the blood of Jesus, his Son, purifies us from all sin.*

God's plan has freed us from our sins as it was God's plan to redeem us and give us hope. Ephesians 1:12, *¹² in order that we, who were the first to hope in Christ, might be for the praise of his glory.* We like it when a well thought out plan comes together, but for us it rarely happens. Rarely do our plans ever end up exactly like we think they will. There are too many variables that can come into play which can alter our plan, but we find hope in knowing God's plan is going to work out according to His plan every single time. This brings a certainty to our hope in Christ.

We find encouragement in knowing that God has a plan and it can improve our daily lives. It improves our lives because we go with God and He goes with us each day. Colossians 1:27, *27 To them God has chosen to make known among the Gentiles the glorious riches of this mystery, which is Christ in you, the hope of glory.* Meditate a moment on the phrase *"Christ in you."* This wonderful truth firms up our hope of God's presence in us.

We have Christ in us and that fills us with His presence. Notice something else from our Ephesian passage. Ephesians 1:13-14, *13 And you also were included in Christ when you heard the word of truth, the gospel of your salvation. Having believed, you were marked in him with a seal, the promised Holy Spirit, 14 who is a deposit guaranteeing our inheritance until the redemption of those who are God's possession – to the praise of his glory.* This seal is the promised Holy Spirit, given to those who obey the salvation gospel. Before we dive into the riches of our inheritance, we must understand we have been given a seal as a mark that assures us of our inheritance.

Each disciple is marked with God's seal and the seal implies ownership. God looks down from heaven and communicates He will take care of us and bless us with an inheritance. We have every reason to be hopeful because God will finish what He started in us. He has given us an earnest guaranteeing our inheritance. The guarantee will not fade as long as we are faithful and let God's Word and the Holy Spirit guide us.

The letter of Acts follows the gospels of Matthew, Mark, Luke, and John. In Acts we read about the gospel that was preached by the apostles concerning Jesus. The gospel they preached following Jesus' death, burial and resurrection, is in itself a summary of the message of hope. 1 Corinthians 15:1-6, *[1] Now, brothers, I want to remind you of the gospel I preached to you, which you received and on which you have taken your stand. [2] By this gospel you are saved, if you hold firmly to the word, I preached to you. Otherwise, you have believed in vain. [3] For what I received I passed on to you as of first importance: that Christ died for our sins according to the Scriptures, [4] that he was buried, that he was raised on the third day according to the Scriptures, [5] and that he appeared to Peter, and then to the Twelve. [6] After that, he appeared to more than five hundred of the brothers at the same time, most of whom are still living, though some have fallen asleep.*

We also learn in Acts how people became Christians by hearing the gospel preached. We also get inspired insight as to when a believer receives the promised Holy Spirit. Acts 2:38-41, *[38] Peter replied, "Repent and be baptized, every one of you, in the name of Jesus Christ for the forgiveness of your sins. And you will receive the gift of the Holy Spirit. [39] The promise is for you and your children and for all who are far off – for all whom the Lord our God will call." [40] With many other words he warned them; and he pleaded with them, "Save yourselves from this corrupt generation." [41] Those who accepted his message were baptized, and about three thousand were added to their number that day.*

We become children of God through faith in Christ when we repent and are baptized into the name of Jesus Christ. At this point not only do we receive the blessing of the remission of sins, we also receive the Holy Spirit as a gift. What a gift God makes available for His people. The Holy Spirit dwells in believers when they accept the message today as they did in Acts 2 on Pentecost.

The apostles were eye witnesses of Jesus before His death on the cross and after His resurrection. Acts 5:32, [32] *We are witnesses of these things, and so is the Holy Spirit, whom God has given to those who obey him.* We have Christ in us. We have the Holy Spirit in us. 1 Corinthians 6:19-20, [19] *Do you not know that your body is a temple of the Holy Spirit, who is in you, whom you have received from God? You are not your own;* [20] *you were bought at a price. Therefore, honor God with your body.*

We can live with a confident hope that comes from living in the presence of God. The Holy Spirit works through God's Word to strengthens us as does Christ. The Divine helps us live faithful Christian lives. Having the Holy Spirit in us and Christ in us does not mean they work against our personal will to live the Christian life.

The Holy Spirit and Jesus help us in our own desire to do the will of God, as we choose to obey God. Romans 8:26-28, [26] *In the same way, the Spirit helps us in our weakness. We do not know what we ought to pray for, but the Spirit himself intercedes for us with groans that words cannot express.* [27] *And he who searches our hearts knows the mind of the Spirit, because the Spirit intercedes for the saints in accordance with God's will.* [28] *And we know that in all things God works for the good of those who love him, who have been called according to his purpose.* We may not understand all of the workings of the Holy Spirit in our lives, but we can be sure God is at work for us and in us.

The Bible says in Philippians 2:13, *[13] It is God who works in you to will and to act according to his good purpose.* The original Greek word translated "works" in our English Bible is the word from which we get the word "energy." God will work in those who have made the decision to follow Jesus. God is working for us today, and in us today, and for us today. Hope comes from trusting that God's presence is at work. This was the point Paul made in Philippians 1:6, *[6] being confident of this, that he who began a good work in you will carry it on to completion until the day of Christ Jesus.*

The seeds of hope are spread through the words found in Ephesians and throughout the Bible. We are told in Luke's gospel that the seed is the Word of God (Luke 8:11). This seed is powerful and if we will let it sink in and be watered it will give us real hope. There are people today who for the longest time did know about any other kind of hope than wishful hope. Perhaps we were unaware of the confident hope that originates from faith in God's Word. Then one day an ever so small seed was thrown in our direction. We found out how God can grow His seed.

Once God's powerful seed takes root and begins to grow in us, life is no longer meaningless. God lovingly and patiently worked His plan, and at some point we made the choice to follow the will and purpose of God for our lives. If so, we are living with hope in a hopeless world. If we are in Christ, we are able to live a no regret kind of life in God's presence.

Let return to the blessing of our spiritual inheritance. Ephesians 1:14, *¹⁴who is a deposit guaranteeing our inheritance until the redemption of those who are God's possession – to the praise of his glory.* The word in Greek translated "deposit" in the New International Version or "earnest" in the King James Version comes from the real estate world.

When we find a house we want to purchase, the seller will require a deposit. It is referred to as "earnest money." The amount of money varies but it is a substantial amount which demonstrates to the seller that we are serious about getting the rest of the funds to buy their home. Our earnest money gives the assurance to the seller that we will accept our responsibility and work towards buying the home.

The work of the Spirit in our lives gives us assurance of our inheritance. When we look at the things that are recorded for us in Ephesians 1:3-14 we cannot help but have hope. We have every spiritual blessing in Christ (1:3). God has made us His chosen people (1:4) and adopted us as His children (1:5). God has redeemed us through the blood of Jesus (1:7). God has granted us forgiveness of sins (1:7). God has lavished on us the riches of His grace (1:7-8). We have been sealed with the Holy Spirit guaranteeing our spiritual inheritance (1:13-14).

The Holy Spirit is our seal of promise that generates an expectant hope and guarantee of our eternal inheritance. Everything else in life may be unstable – our health, our family, our job, our education, our society, and everything else we see in our world. We may feel like we are out on a ledge of a high-rise building and the wind is blowing and we are trying to keep balance.

God wants us to have stability in this unstable world so He guarantees our spiritual inheritance. All the material possessions in the world cannot compare with our inheritance in Christ. As we continue our *Journey into a Hope-Filled Life* we will learn more reasons to live with hope in a world that is often filled with hopelessness.

CHAPTER 2 – QUESTIONS
TO DISCUSS, DEVELOP, AND DETERMINE

1. What concept or idea is associated with the Greek word redemption?

2. What does the Greek word for forgiveness represent in Ephesians?

3. What did the living goat that was sent outside of the camp on the Day of Atonement remind the people in Israel? What common English word is based on this event?

4. How does 2 Corinthians 5:21 explain how we can live in God's presence? How do these two passages, 1 Corinthians 6:19 and Colossians 1:27, support our belief that God's presence is living in us?

5. God worked His plan so we could have what kind of fellowship? What was unique about the kind of fellowship God had with Adam and Eve in the garden?

6. When do we receive the seal of the Holy Spirit and what does the seal represent? What does the seal of the Holy Spirit assure us?

7. The Holy Spirit helps us in our desire to do what? How does meaning marked with the Holy Spirit strengthen our hope in Christ?

8. Name three truths we can take away from Hebrews 9:27-28.

Chapter 3

Prayer is mentioned more times than HS in the Bible

FIND HOPE IN GOD'S PRAYING PEOPLE
(Ephesians 1:15-19a, 3:14-16, 6:18-20)

Prayers of the faithful move God – that is exciting to even think about. God has been busy working in many of our lives through prayer. We pray for God to deliver us from temptation. We pray for God to provide our daily bread. We pray God to help us in our times of trial. We pray for our friends and their friends asking God to intervene in their situations. It is always right to pray and God wants us to pray at all times.

God wants to hear from us all the time. However, the only time He hears from some people is when they have tried everything else and nothing else has worked, so they finally seek God's help through prayer. The amazing thing about the last resort approach to prayer is that God still stands ready to hear them. Unfortunately, when we delay our prayers, we miss out on some of the blessings we could have known earlier simply because we have not prayed on all occasions.

In our battles against sin and trials do we practice prayer as a last resort, or does our prayer life reflect a daily dependence on God? Ephesians 6:18, *And pray in the Spirit on all occasions with all kinds of prayers and requests. With this in mind, be alert and always keep on praying for all the saints.* If we will pray on all occasions we will be alert and ready for whatever our spiritual enemy throws in our path.

The impact of our prayer's springs heaven into action. Psalm 34:7, *The angel of the LORD encamps around those who fear him, and he delivers them.*

An old story has been circulated among preachers of a little boy who certainly believed in prayer. The little boy was in a church assembly and he just would not be still in his mother's arms. He was squirming and talking out loud and disrupting those seated around him. After several warnings, his mother passed him on to her husband and he picked him up, and tucked him under his arm, and started to exit the assembly. As they neared the back of the auditorium, the boy screamed out in a loud voice, "Please, please pray for me!"

The boy had not quite learned how to act in a church assembly, but at least he had learned something about prayer. We need to pray not only for ourselves, but we also need to petition others to pray for us. It is significant that the great apostle Paul prayed not only for his readers and for their spiritual blessings, but he also requested their prayers. Ephesians 6:19-20, [19] *Pray also for me, that whenever I open my mouth, words may be given me so that I will fearlessly make known the mystery of the gospel, [20] for which I am an ambassador in chains. Pray that I may declare it fearlessly, as I should.*

As a Christian and one of God's chosen apostles, Paul suffered a great deal for Christ in his efforts to share the good news with others. He was "an ambassador in chains." The idea is noteworthy. Paul had spent his fair share of time in jail, or confined in prison, for doing nothing more than trying to spread the news of Jesus and His resurrection. 2 Corinthians 5:20, *We are therefore Christ's ambassadors, as though God were making his appeal through us. We implore you on Christ's behalf: Be reconciled to God.*

Paul chose to follow Christ because he understood there was no eternal hope in this world without being reconciled to God. The people around Paul knew he was serious about being with God in heaven, and he thanked God for the Christians who joined in the missionary efforts to spread the good news of everlasting hope. Ephesians 1:15-16, *[15] For this reason, ever since I heard about your faith in the Lord Jesus and your love for all the saints, [16] I have not stopped giving thanks for you, remembering you in my prayers.*

It is not unusual for Paul to talk about prayer in his letters. However, it is a bit unusual for him to break into prayer in the midst of a letter as he does at some length both here in Ephesians 1:15 and in Ephesians 3:14. It is clearly out of Paul's love for the Lord and his fellow Christians that he burst out in praise and prayer. Paul mentioned the thanksgiving he continually gave for the Lord's disciples. He was deeply grateful for them and constantly brought them before God in prayer (1:16).

In Paul's efforts to help people know God, he depended on God to provide him power through prayer. Ephesians 1:17-19a, *[17] I keep asking that the God of our Lord Jesus Christ, the glorious Father, may give you the Spirit of wisdom and revelation, so that you may know him better. [18] I pray also that the eyes of your heart may be enlightened in order that you may know the hope to which he has called you, the riches of his glorious inheritance in the saints,* [19a] *and his incomparably great power for us who believe.*

Paul prayed on behalf of the saints, and in so doing he gave us a model of how we can pray for one another. He wanted them to get to know God better. The Bible is a love story of the God who wants to be known and who wants to bless us. God wants us to know Him and He gives us the grace that allows us to grow in our knowledge of Him. By knowing Him we can know hope; this hope is not available to those who do not know God or forget God. Job 8:13b, *the hope of the godless shall perish* (English Standard Version).

It does not matter how long we have been a Christian; if we let go of knowing Christ better, Satan will work into our heart and we will become stagnant in our relationship with God. If we are not battling with Satan at some level, we are likely not growing as a Christian. Satan hates it when we are making decisions that helps us grow. Satan does not like it when we resolve in our heart to know Christ better – in fact, he gets extremely mad.

We can know Christ better through prayer. Communication is a necessary ingredient to any ongoing, healthy relationship. We are not going to have a strong relationship with someone we rarely talk to. I am always happy when my children call me, for it brings a smile to my face, and I know it brings a smile to the face of God when we talk to Him. There are rich blessings that come our way from simply talking to God.

We can know Christ better by reading His Word – the Bible. As we seek to know Christ better our goal must be to develop His heart in us. When we desire to better understand His love, His strength, and the hope He wants to pour into our lives as Christians, we are blessed beyond measure. This is why Paul prayed in Ephesians 3:18-19 that we know God's immeasurable love. By reading the Bible we come to realize that being a Christian is the greatest thing in all the world!

To know the hope and the inheritance, Paul used a phrase that appears only here in the entire Bible. He prayed *that the eyes of their hearts will be enlightened so that they will understand the hope to which they have been called* (1:18). Paul was not talking about the organ that pumps blood to the body. Along with other Biblical writers, he used "heart" to refer to that deepest part of man. He was praying here that at the very core of who they were, they would have spiritual eyes wide open to see what a profound hope all Christians have.

Specifically, he wanted them to grasp *"the riches of his glorious inheritance in the saints."* To be confident about the inheritance that is coming to the faithful is to be secure in our hope. Our weaknesses and the unpredictability of life can make us feel insecure and uncertain. God wants us to know His eternal security and see clearly that we are headed for a rich inheritance.

I remember the first time I became the owner of a pair of prescription eyeglasses. I was a student in Bible school and I found myself struggling to see the notes projected on the board from the overhead projector. OK, so that dates me a bit. Anyway, I humbled myself and went to the eye doctor. I did not want to admit I could not see as well as those people sitting around me in class, but I wanted to get the notes right so I could also pass the tests in the course.

At the time I felt I could see ok in other areas of my life, but I was strongly encouraged by my teacher to get my eyes checked. I mention strongly because the suggestion came with the admonition if I wanted to have a chance of passing his class, I better get some glasses. Well I had a plan. I would wear them to see the blackboard and the overhead transparences, but then they would be off my face before I would leave his classroom. Therefore, the only people that would have to see me in these new found spectacles were those in my class and this particular teacher.

That was my plan before I got the glasses, but my plan changed in a matter of one day. When I put on my glasses for the first time, I discovered to my utter amazement that the world surely looked good in focus. I had not realized what I had been missing outside of the class notes. The green leaves on the trees had a much deeper color than I had been seeing. All kinds of beautiful and distinct colors came into my focus. The colors were a great deal deeper and richer everywhere I looked, compared to the blurry blobs of color I had been observing.

The world in focus was far more exciting than the world I had been seeing! Then how much more beautiful and hope-filled could we be if we could see through the eyes of Christ. That is why Paul prayed for us to enlighten the eyes of our hearts so we can know the hope God extends to us. Even though we are still in the midst of the Christian adventure, with the eyes of our heart we can see the end of the video – and we can see "in Christ" we are winners!

If we want the Scripture to come alive to us, we must in ever-increasing ways seek to know Christ better. Knowing Christ better involves letting God's truth transform our hearts. Let us live not only as those who look through heaven's eyes, but also as those who clearly have heaven's hope in their eyes. This hope opens us up to new horizons of the riches of our inheritance. We do not hope for heaven as many in the world wishfully hope. We have a firm hope we are on our way to heaven so we naturally sing out our praise to God's glory.

Paul prayed for a host of wonderful things for the saints in Ephesians 1. In verse 18 he repeated the idea of our having an inheritance that he mentioned earlier in Ephesians 1:14. This time he referred to it as a *glorious inheritance* (1:18). We spoke to this idea in the previous chapter so let us pay more careful attention to the other things found in verse 18.

Paul wanted his readers to *"know the hope"* to which God had called them. This is the true hope that is bolstered with confidence because of our relationship with Christ. This is the hope we can know when we start seeing things the way God sees them. This is the hope we can know when we start seeing the eternal instead of only what our eyes can physically see. This is the hope that has a foundation that will stand eternal because it stems from God to God's people. This is the hope I have seen in countless Christians over the years.

This is the hope that allows a person to see beyond their current troubles to their glorious inheritance. Romans 5:3-5, *³ Not only so, but we also rejoice in our sufferings, because we know that suffering produces perseverance; ⁴ perseverance, character; and character, hope. ⁵ And hope does not disappoint us, because God has poured out his love into our hearts by the Holy Spirit, whom he has given us.* God does not cause all the suffering we see in this world. Life sometimes hurts because we live in a sinful world. Satan is very much active, and yet there is much we can learn to appreciate in our times of suffering.

Suffering can harvest some godly qualities in our lives. Perseverance and character are refined by how we handle suffering. If we have the enlightened eyes to see as Paul prayed for us to have in Ephesians 1:18, we will have hope. We need a certain mindset to understand and appreciate God's process that brings hope. Our hope grows stronger when our minds continue to trust God, follow His Word, and focus on eternal matters. Praying people are people who have come to know the hope that is filled with the riches of God's eternal blessings.

Bible hope is the blessed hope that propels us forward through all kinds of obstacles. People with this kind of hope think differently because this hope is connected to love and faith. Colossians 1:3-5, *³ We always thank God, the Father of our Lord Jesus Christ, when we pray for you, ⁴ because we have heard of your faith in Christ Jesus and of the love you have for all the saints – ⁵ the faith and love that spring from the hope that is stored up for you in heaven and that you have already heard about in the word of truth, the gospel.*

Hope that is stored for us in heaven is none other than a glorious hope. Hope has a resting place in heaven.

We can have confidence in the everlasting hope because it is reserved for us in heaven. This hope will help us endure all kinds of hardships and sufferings here because we know we are on our way to heaven. Paul tried to encourage his coworker Timothy in the trials he was facing or would face by reminding him of the trials Paul faced in his own ministry for the Lord. 2 Timothy 3:10-15, *[10] You, however, know all about my teaching, my way of life, my purpose, faith, patience, love, endurance, [11] persecutions, sufferings – what kinds of things happened to me in Antioch, Iconium and Lystra, the persecutions I endured. Yet the Lord rescued me from all of them. [12] In fact, everyone who wants to live a godly life in Christ Jesus will be persecuted, [13] while evil men and impostors will go from bad to worse, deceiving and being deceived. [14] But as for you, continue in what you have learned and have become convinced of, because you know those from whom you learned it, [15] and how from infancy you have known the holy Scriptures, which are able to make you wise for salvation through faith in Christ Jesus.*

God's Word is our GPS that leads us to salvation. Paul prayed not only for Timothy, but for all his fellow servants of Christ, to stay on the track of faith no matter what kinds of sufferings they met along the way. Paul wanted the church in Ephesus and other places to know that he constantly went before the throne room of God in their behalf. Prayer helps us to remain faithful, so let us pray with confidence. Hebrews 4:16, *Let us then approach the throne of grace with confidence, so that we may receive mercy and find grace to help us in our time of need.*

Hebrews 3:12-14, *[12] See to it, brothers, that none of you has a sinful, unbelieving heart that turns away from the living God. [13] But encourage one another daily, as long as it is called Today, so that none of you may be hardened by sin's deceitfulness. [14] We have come to share in Christ if we hold firmly till the end the confidence, we had at first.* Israel of old erred in their hearts because they chose unbelief. They did not believe God would give them victory in Canaan even though they had seen God do great things in Egypt. The people of Israel erred in their hearts and lost hope.

The heart of every spiritual problem is a problem of the heart, and perhaps that is why Paul prayed for the hearts of those in the church to be enlightened to the blessing of the hope of our calling. Hope helps us keep upright in this upside-down world. God's hope-filled Word can keep us from drifting away from the hope we have found in Christ. Hebrews 2:1-3, *[1] We must pay more careful attention, therefore, to what we have heard, so that we do not drift away. [2] For if the message spoken by angels was binding, and every violation and disobedience received its just punishment, [3] how shall we escape if we ignore such a great salvation? This salvation, which was first announced by the Lord, was confirmed to us by those who heard him.*

If we leave Christ there is no salvation nor hope for us. Hebrews 4:1, *Therefore, since the promise of entering his rest still stands, let us be careful that none of you be found to have fallen short of it.* Let us be a people who will always say "yes" to God. In this way we know God will be with us and help us as we cross our rivers of trial and fight our giant problems whatever they may be. If we pray for ourselves and those who are following Christ, we are well on the way to enjoying the hope stored up for us in heaven.

Paul's prayer in Ephesians chapter 1 and chapter 3 mentions we have been blessed with God's power at work in us. Ephesians 3:14-16, *[14] For this reason I kneel before the Father, [15] from whom his whole family in heaven and on earth derives its name. [16] I pray that out of his glorious riches he may strengthen you with power through his Spirit in your inner being.* Paul spoke of how God's power enabled him to do the things God had called him to do. Philippians 4:13, *I can do everything through him who gives me strength.*

Paul acknowledged he could do all things through Christ because God's power was at work in him. And he emphasized in his prayers for the Christians to let God's power work in them. We will dig deeper in the next chapter in this book on the subject of resurrection power. At this point we should nail down this important truth in our hearts – there is great power for us who believe.

The Bible gives us the assurance we have been given power. The power that is available to us is practical power. Practical power is the power that can help us in our time of need. The Lord told us how we should pray and tap into God's power in our battle against temptation. Matthew 6:13, *And lead us not into temptation, but deliver us from the evil one.* When we pray this prayer, it is a request for strength to be led away from yielding to temptation and falling to the enemy of our soul.

Are we lonely? Pray. Are we frightened? Pray. Are we treated unfairly? Pray. Are we thankful? Pray. Are we suffering? Pray. What do we do when we find ourselves in a lion's den and we are not hunting lions? Pray. We pray because we can know God is our only hope for this life and eternity. We pray knowing God cares and this alone strengthens our hope.

I want to mention something important about our prayers that I have not emphasized to this point. We are to pray not only for those in Christ, but we should also pray for those outside of Christ. We should include in our prayers those who are living without true hope. We should pray that they may come to know the hope of being in the care of Jesus in this life and look forward to the future hope. When Paul prayed in Ephesians 6:19-20, he was asking the church to pray for him that he might help others to come to know the good news of Jesus.

When I first met a fellow by the name of John, he already had cancer. One thing that impressed me from our first visit was his upbeat attitude with me in his bad situation. I was a bit surprised with the kind reception he gave me after I introduced myself. I mention this because his sister, who was a Christian, had tried to get him to agree to visit with me for several years, but he had always declined a visit. His sister thought after he was first diagnosed with cancer, he might agree to let me come and talk with him. However, he told his sister to tell me he had no interest in visiting with her preacher.

During that time his sister said, "Clark, all we can do is keep praying for him and that he will eventually agree to talk with someone about death and eternity." Ephesians 1:17, *I keep asking that the God of our Lord Jesus Christ, the glorious Father, may give you the Spirit of wisdom and revelation, so that you may know him better.* His sister knew Paul's prayer in Ephesians was directed toward Christians but she wanted her brother to know God better, much better, than he did.

A few years went by in her brother's battle with cancer and for the most part he had done fairly well with his serious health issues. During this time, he remained unwilling to visit with me, but he eventually told her he would appreciate my praying for him. She had told him we had been praying for him in our congregation for a long time. She was pleased to see he was receptive and appreciative of our prayers.

One day his health took a turn for the worse and things became more intense. He had been in and out of the hospital dozens of times before he finally agreed for me to visit. When I walked into his hospital room to meet him for the first time, I did not know much about his religious background or exactly where he was spiritually in his life. All I knew for sure was he had been unwilling for me, the preacher, to visit him until now.

Since I did not know where he was in his spiritual journey, I asked John in our first visit if he felt good about where he was spiritually. He acted confident and his attitude seemed good in that he was willing to talk about death and eternity. He talked and I listened. Sometimes that is the best thing we can do is to listen.

John spoke to me that he felt that spiritually he was in a good place. I said something like that was good to hear. He seemed to have found a measure of peace during this difficult time. However, knowing that John needed to know Jesus better I went on to say, "John if it is all right with you, I would like to visit you again and get to know you." He had no reservations on my visiting him in the hospital.

I felt like he really meant what he had said to me about visiting him. In the days to follow I learned that he truly did want me to visit him. I concluded my first visit with John with a prayer. Following the prayer, I said, "John, if you ever have any questions about the Bible or spiritual things, I would like you to give me an opportunity to open the Bible with you and look with you for the answers."

It was not long before John started asking some questions and one question led to another and it seemed his interest in God was growing in our discussions. We know faith comes from hearing and it appeared that his faith was growing as we discussed various things. John's faith came into focus in the next couple of months. One day I received a call from the specialty hospital; it was John. John wanted to be baptized into Christ. He wanted to have the hope of God's pleasure and know the hope of God's presence.

In addition to his physical family that loved him, he found the strength that God provides in His spiritual family, the church. John's family prayed, the church prayed, and John became a believer in prayer. He would tell people that he believed God had helped him not to suffer as much pain as one might think one would experience in his condition. He understood that God had created him as an eternal being to live forever, just not here on this earth.

Because of his faith in God John was able to leave this life with no regrets. God had a hold of John and John lived with hope in what appeared to be a hopeless situation. John felt the strength of God from his bed and the love of his family from his bed even in his final hour. John wrestled with his cancer, but he still lived a life of no regrets. His outlook was proof that cancer cannot erode hope, love, faith, or peace.

Cancer cannot destroy confidence or kill friendship or family relationships or shut out precious memories or silence courage. John's faith illuminated brightly during his final days on earth. Even in his weakened state John wanted prayer, and when I prayed, he would join in with me by saying "Amen!" He wanted to hear spiritual songs and hymns and those who prayed those prayers and sang those songs were themselves reassured that John had lived a life of no regrets.

John did not accept something or believe something simply because others believed it. It was apparent John not only wrestled with his cancer, but in a way, he wrestled with his faith. There is an interesting story in Genesis 32 that takes place by the river Jabbok. In that chapter of the Bible we find the Patriarch Jacob had come to wrestle with God, but God was there to teach Jacob he needed to rely on God's strength, not his own. God did not give up on Jacob and we are thankful today because God does not give up on us.

John certainly wrestled with his cancer – he never wanted to give up. But in his struggle, through God's Word he came to sense the presence of the God who had come to wrestle with him. The God who knew Jacob by his name – knew

John's name. In all of John's trials as a Christian there were no visual signs of any real good physical news, but his faith never wavered nor did he give up on God. Cancer did not defeat John because that disease could not steal his hope or his faith.

Believers can live with hope and experience a "no regrets" kind of life. A no regrets life leads us to a no regrets eternity. The Apostle Paul wrote in his final days, *Now there is in store for me the crown of righteousness, which the Lord, the righteous Judge, will award to me on that day – and not only to me, but also to all who have longed for his appearing* (2 Timothy 4:8).

What is important in life is that we come to know God. John 17:3, *Now this is eternal life: that they may know you, the only true God, and Jesus Christ, whom you have sent.* John's life was a testimony to this truth. John was an honest, hard-working man. He worked by the sweat of his brow. His labors gained for him and his family a good life, not always an easy life but certainly a good life. But instead of patting himself on the back and proudly pointing to all that he had accomplished, he came to understand that the really important things in life are not those things we gain by our own labors but those things given to us as gifts from the heavenly Father.

Ephesians is a reminder how we can find hope in God's praying people. I mentioned already that when I first met John, I mainly listened to him. I do think that listening is the best thing we can do sometimes; although we do have to open our mouth at some point to help people come to know God better. By truly listening to a person, coupled with our actions and words, he can see whether or not we sincerely care.

I imagine we have all heard the phrase, "With friends like these you don't need enemies." I do not know where this phrase originated, but the story of Job definitely reminds me of the phrase. The phrase reminds me of the three friends who came to Job during his severe trial and they did not say anything for seven days. The story within the story of Job teaches us the value of listening or being quiet when we are trying to encourage our sick or suffering friends. It communicates to us the value of proper actions and it also reminds us of the power of our words.

We can speak foolishly and flippantly, or we can speak hope-filled words that flow from knowing God. The first good thing Job's friends did for him was to come to him during his time of suffering. Job 2:11, *When Job's three friends, Eliphaz the Temanite, Bildad the Shuhite and Zophar the Naamathite, heard about all the troubles that had come upon him, they set out from their homes and met together by agreement to go and sympathize with him and comfort him.* It was soothing for Job to see his friends by his side.

Job 2:13, *Then they sat on the ground with him for seven days and seven nights. No one said a word to him, because they saw how great his suffering was.* The second-best thing they did was surround him in silence as they could see the evidence of his severe suffering. However, his friends muted the two good things they had done for Job when they finally opened their mouths. They said hurtful and incorrect things out of their own ignorance of God.

All three friends spoke foolishly and implied horrible things. There was even the accusation Job was suffering because of his own sins and wrong doing. We know they were wrong! Job 1:8, *Then the LORD said to Satan, "Have you considered my servant Job? There is no one on earth like him; he is blameless and upright, a man who fears God and shuns evil."* God's view of Job was the accurate view. His suffering was not due to his sin. His friends' inaccurate view of God and Job would keep them from praying with faith for Job. It would also keep them from the hope that resided in Job's heart during his trials.

When we know the character of Job, it is no surprise that he held onto his hope in God through his mental, emotional, and intense physical suffering. There are no less than ten prayers in Job. The word "hope" is found seventeen times in Job. Job 13:15, *Though he slays me, yet will I hope in him; I will surely defend my ways to his face.* Job 27:8, *For what hope has the godless when he is cut off, when God takes away his life?* Thank God, Job left us a great example of how we can live with hope in the midst of devastating tragedy or severe suffering.

We can find hope in prayer and God's praying people. Job prayed in his suffering, but this man who feared God undoubtedly prayed before his days of suffering. We all experience some degree of suffering. It is so prevalent in our world and what people need in their trials, is hope – biblical hope. There is nothing good about the suffering cancer can bring on a person and a family. Cancer or any other ugly word that might cause us to suffer may cause us to ask ourselves the "Why?" question. Why does God allow suffering? We are not given much of an answer to our why questions in life.

We can know the Lord Himself, a man without any sin, suffered so we might be eternally blessed. We can know from Scripture that we live in a sin-filled world, but we are headed for a perfect world with God. We can know suffering in this world comes to the just and the unjust. We can know that God cares for all people and in His care of not wanting anyone to perish (2 Peter 3:9) He provides hope of eternal life (Titus 3:7). Our prayers can strengthen our hope and trust in God during our suffering. That is the example Job gives us.

There is great value in listening coupled with proper actions and proper words. I listened to John that first day. He could tell I was really listening. He had previously been told his sister's church family and the preacher had been praying for him. He did not know that I had prayed right before I walked into his hospital room that first day. I believe my prayer to God led me to intently listen to John. By listening carefully, I was given a chance to eventually speak words of hope to him; and he listened intently.

I firmly believe the many prayers that had been offered up for John contributed to his having the opportunity not only to hear the good news of Jesus but also to respond by faith to the hope-filled message of Jesus. The message of hope left John with no regrets. We should follow the example of Paul and pray that we would open our eyes so we can know God better. We devote ourselves to prayer so we can understand the fullness of God in our inner being and claim our hope and extend hope to others.

1. What are the advantages of praying on all occasions as mentioned in Ephesians 6:18? Why did Paul ask the church in Ephesus to pray for him?

2. What was the goal of Paul's prayerful words in Ephesians 1:17 for the believers? Name two ways we can accomplish this goal or fulfill the purpose of his prayer in verse 17.

3. Why does Paul pray for their eyes to be enlightened in Ephesians 1:18?

4. How can our hope in God grow stronger? Name two things for which Paul prayed that springs forth from hope. (see Colossians 1:5)

5. What is the practical power available for Christians as they pray? How did Paul explain the strengthening power of God in his life? (see Philippians 4:13)

6. In addition to prayer what is the best thing we can sometimes do in our effort to try to help others know Jesus better? What did Jesus say eternal life was in John's gospel?

7. What three things did Job's friends do in his suffering? Explain the good, the bad, and the ugly.

8. How have you been encouraged by the prayers of someone else or from the prayers in the church family?

FIND HOPE IN GOD'S POWER
(Ephesians 1:19-23, 3:16-17a, 3:20-21, 6:10)

There is power and then there is resurrection power. I have heard the following story be told in various versions by several preachers over the years. It does make an effective point in light of the subject emphasis in this chapter. A woman happened to be looking out of her window at home one day when she saw her German shepherd shaking the life out of her neighbor's pet rabbit. She was horrified so she grabbed a broom and ran outside and started pushing the dog with her broom until he finally let go of the rabbit.

Sadly, the rabbit was covered with the saliva from her dog and at this point she realized the rabbit was dead. The woman lifted the rabbit by the ears and took it inside and washed all the blood and saliva off of the rabbit under her sink faucet. She did this because the relationship between her and her neighbor had been strained for years. After realizing what her dog had done to her neighbor's pet rabbit, instead of confessing what had happened to her neighbor's pet, she devised a plan.

After cleaning up the dead rabbit she dried the rabbit off with a towel and then used her blow dryer. She fluffed the hair left on the rabbit the best she could with a comb. After she groomed the rabbit she waited until her neighbor was not looking and she hopped over the fence and propped the rabbit up in his cage. About an hour later the woman with the plan heard a loud scream coming from her neighbor's back yard. She ran out into her backyard pretending she did not know what was going on and asked her neighbor what happened.

Her neighbor came over to the fence and said, "Our rabbit is back – our rabbit's back!" Her neighbor asked, "What do you mean he's back?" She said, "Our rabbit died a week ago and we buried him in the creek bank behind our fence, but I looked out the window a minute ago and I saw our rabbit sitting up in his cage!" Who can deny the significant power of resurrection? Resurrection grabs your attention – even if it is a rabbit.

There is power and then there is resurrection power. What a blessing it is to believe in the resurrection power of Jesus and to know it is at work in us who believe. Ephesians 1:19-23, *[19] and his incomparably great power for us who believe. That power is like the working of his mighty strength, [20] which he exerted in Christ when he raised him from the dead and seated him at his right hand in the heavenly realms, [21] far above all rule and authority, power and dominion, and every title that can be given, not only in the present age but also in the one to come. [22] And God placed all things under his feet and appointed him to be head over everything for the church, [23] which is his body, the fullness of him who fills everything in every way.*

If people are not fully convinced that Christ has the power coupled with the desire to deliver them from Satan's pull, they will lose hope and continue down the meaningless cycle of life. If people do not have a proper view of Jesus it is no wonder why the ground is sinking below them. There is only one foundation in life that lasts and that is the life built on the authority, power, and dominion of the awe-inspiring Creator God.

Whatever evil forces are seeking to wreak havoc in our lives and hold us back, bog us down, and spin our wheels, we must, remember these forces do not have all authority and power. The spiritual forces of evil do not have power over our spiritual life or death. The fact that runs through Scripture is that our spiritual enemy is no match for God's Almighty power that now works in us who believe.

Evil cannot destroy what God has given us in Christ or take away our inheritance unless we choose to turn away from God's resurrection type of power. We can enjoy God's power at work in us and believe God will work all things for our eternal good. Not all things are good, but God is good. God's power did not spare Joseph from prison in Genesis 39, but God's power did get him through this difficult time. And in time Joseph was blessed to be in charge of that very prison.

God's power did not prevent Moses from being exiled in Midian, but by God's power Moses was able to stand up to Pharaoh with mighty miracles and deliver God's people from their bondage in Egypt. God's power did not prevent Jairus' daughter from dying in Matthew 9, but by God's power she was raised to life. God's power did not prevent Bartimaeus from being born blind, but by God's power his sight was restored (Mark 10). God's power did not prevent Paul and Silas from being beaten and thrown in jail in the city of Philippi, but by God's power their chains came loose and salvation came to the house of the Philippian jailer (Acts 16).

God is the ultimate power in the universe. When we make the decision to follow Jesus, we become connected to the source above all sources, to the power above all powers, to the name above all names. Christians are joined with the most powerful force in the universe – God Almighty! The Bible reveals that in Jesus' presence the weak became strong and the helpless found hope in Him.

The Bible reveals that one of the most amazing things about God's power is that it can be at work in us. His power brings hope into our troubling situations. God's resurrection power can help us from yielding to temptation. It can help us live victoriously over our spiritual enemy which we will explore in detail in the last chapter of this book. At this point just note that Ephesians 6:10 tells us, *Finally, be strong in the Lord and in his mighty power*. The same power that raised Jesus from the dead is available to us.

Power was an emphasis in Paul's prayers. Ephesians 3:16-17a, *I pray that out of his glorious riches he may strengthen you with power through his Spirit in your inner being, [17a] so that Christ may dwell in your hearts through faith.*

Ephesians 3:20-21, *[20] Now to him who is able to do immeasurably more than all we ask or imagine, according to his power that is at work within us, [21] to him be glory in the church and in Christ Jesus throughout all generations, for ever and ever! Amen.*

We should not forget there is no one higher or more powerful in all of history than Jesus Christ. Jesus' resume was unlike anyone else's, being exalted to the highest place. Philippians 2:9-11, *9 "Therefore God exalted him to the highest place and gave him the name that is above every name, 10 that at the name of Jesus every knee should bow, in heaven and on earth and under the earth, 11 and every tongue confess that Jesus Christ is Lord, to the glory of God the Father."*

What exactly did Jesus, who has a name that is far above every other name, do according to Philippians? He voluntarily humbled himself and suffered death on the cross, so that by His sacrifice we might live forever with Him. The cross proves how much Jesus wants to have a relationship with all of us. His resurrection three days later proves He can make that happen!

Paul who wrote both the Philippian and Ephesian letters desired to know all he could about Christ. He wanted to experience the mighty resurrection power of God in his own life. Paul stated it this way in Philippians 3:10, *I want to know Christ and the power of his resurrection and the fellowship of sharing in his sufferings, becoming like him in his death.* Paul wanted others to know Christ fully and the hope found by living in the power of His resurrection. The Christian journey is fueled by Jesus' death, burial and glorious resurrection.

The resurrection of Jesus grabs our attention, solidifies our hope, and changes our lives. God wants to strengthen us with spiritual power. When God's power is working in our inner being, we will have spiritual strength. The "inner man" or "inner being" in Ephesians 3:16 refers to the spiritual man that directs our thoughts, actions, and motives. The inner man strength God provides us fuels our minds with the passionate desire to do God's will. It provides us the energy to do what is right in God's eyes regardless of the people around us doing wrong.

My watch runs on a battery for a while, but after several days I can see the warning signs that tells me I need to charge it again. The watch signals that the energy is almost gone and if I desire to keep being able to tell the time I have no choice but to supply it with more energy. We all have devices like our computers or cell phones that will warn us that it is time to recharge the device.

It does not matter how optimistic we may be about these devices that run on energy, there comes a point in time when my watch, phone, or the cordless drill will no longer work without tapping into power. Of course, we do not function on batteries, but we do have a limited amount of internal energy regardless of our desire to keep going. God designed us to refuel and recharge our bodies and our minds with rest.

How does God refill our energy tanks? God does so by giving us physical rest and physical nourishment, but He also gives us spiritual rest and spiritual nourishment. Jesus will give us rest and strength from the situations that wear us down. He will give us rest from our sins that have worn us out. Jesus encourages us to rest in Him. *Come to me, all you who are weary and burdened, and I will give you rest* (Matthew 11:28).

How does Jesus fill us up when we are running on empty? He does so by inviting us to rest in Him and plug our faith into His resurrection power. God wants to strengthen us with His power. The purpose of our being strengthened through His Spirit in our inner being is so Christ may "dwell" in our hearts through faith (Ephesians 3:17a). There are two words in the original language that can be translated "dwell." One means to stay at a place on a temporary basis, like a hotel; the other means to "settle down." It is the difference between a hotel and a home.

The Greek word (KATOIKEO) used in Ephesians 3:17 means to "settle down." Paul prayed for God to have a permanent residency in our hearts. Jesus does not simply want to be a guest in our hearts, He wants to take up permanent residence. God's goal is to strengthen us with power so Christ may dwell in our hearts through faith.

We must not overlook the words "by faith" or "through faith" in Ephesians 3:17. The Lord wants to dwell in our hearts through faith. Faith comes from hearing God's Word, so it is our responsibility to hear the Word and let it sink down inside to our hearts. The power available to Christians through the Spirit works in correlation with our appetite for the Word.

We get spiritual energy as we refill our tanks with God's Almighty Word. Jesus shared these insightful words as He began His ministry. *Blessed are those who hunger and thirst for righteousness, for they will be filled* (Matthew 5:6). This hunger and thirst points to a famished hunger or an unquenchable thirst for righteousness. It is a hungering and thirsting for the whole loaf of righteousness, not just a slice of the loaf.

My wife's grandmother used to make the best dinner rolls in the world. When she would make those rolls, that is all I wanted to eat at family gatherings. It did not matter what else was there to eat – I wanted to fill my plate with those delicious rolls. I would go back for seconds and my seconds consisted of more of her rolls. I smelled them before I ever saw them and then I sought out after them. I hungered for granny's great dinner rolls.

We all have had our own experiences with food and those things our mother or grandmother made for us. When Jesus talked about hunger in Matt. 5:6, He was not referring to a condition that can be satisfied by grandmother's dinner rolls, pies, or some other dish. Instead the hunger and thirst have an object, "righteousness."

The filling or satisfaction in Matthew 5:6, is not at all limited to God's ability. This filling is tied to an individual's appetite. God is able to fill and satisfy us to the full if we have the right appetite for righteousness. When we hunger and thirst for righteousness, it moves us beyond the place of simply information about God, but to a process of transformation by God.

Our hope in God and the power we can enjoy in our inner being is connected in some measure to our spiritual appetite. The appetite we possess for God's righteousness will determine our desire to follow God. The desire we have for God will determine what we do for God. In fact, our desire for God will determine our hope in God.

Most of us have at one time or another sat down on the seat of a bicycle and peddled our way down the street. We probably never watched a video on how to ride a bicycle or attended a seminar on the subject. So how did we learn to ride a bicycle? We learned to ride a bicycle by learning to ride! At first, we may have scraped our knees and dented our pride, but gradually we wobbled down the road and got the hang of it. The reason we learned how to ride a bicycle was because we wanted to ride a bicycle.

If our desire was strong enough and we could get our hands on a bike somewhere, we learned to ride by riding. We could talk about it and ask others about it and get the basic information, but if our desire was to ride a bike there came a point where we had to actually climb on the bike and start peddling. In some ways, faith is like that.

Understanding the theory of righteousness will not take us to the place of filling. Talking about righteousness will not get us there; at some point in time we have to have the internal desire to climb on the teaching Jesus teaches His followers and peddle. The forward progress we can make comes by faith. Although Christ wants to dwell in our hearts, our desire will determine whether or not we allow Him to take up permanent residence or limit Him to an occasional visit.

God's resurrection power is at work in our inner being when our faith and hope is in God. Jesus had told His disciples the news ahead of time, but understandably they did not digest the news. Matthew 16:21, *From that time on Jesus began to explain to his disciples that he must go to Jerusalem and suffer many things at the hands of the elders, chief priests and teachers of the law, and that he must be killed and on the third day be raised to life.*

Jesus predicted the events that would unfold, but they still did not understand. Matthew 20:17-19, *[17] Now as Jesus was going up to Jerusalem, he took the twelve disciples aside and said to them, [18] "We are going up to Jerusalem, and the Son of Man will be betrayed to the chief priests and the teachers of the law. They will condemn him to death [19] and will turn him over to the Gentiles to be mocked and flogged and crucified. On the third day he will be raised to life!"*

Jesus disciples expected a king, but got a martyr. They struggled to absorb what Jesus had told about what was going to happen even before it happened. Nonetheless, Jesus was headed to Calvary where He would die on a cross so He could become the atoning sacrifice for our sins (1 John 4:10). The soldiers came to arrest Jesus while he was with his disciples in the olive grove. The soldiers were being guided by Judas, the betrayer in the darkness of the night. It was dark except for the lit torches and lanterns some were carrying. The soldiers came to do the task which they had been ordered to do.

Peter pulled his sword and cut off the ear of the high priest's servant (John 18:10). Jesus told Peter to put away his sword and in front of them all He healed the man's ear (Luke 22:51). The miracle maker healed again in the presence of the confused minds of His disciples, the hard hearts of the chief priests and Pharisees, and the bewildered soldiers. Jesus knew it was time. He had recently prayed these words to the Father. *Father, the time has come. Glorify your Son, that your Son may glorify you* (John 17:1b).

Jesus refused to put up any resistance to being led away by the detachment of soldiers. This is not at all what the disciples thought should be happening. Where was Jesus the king? Where was the one who was going to lead them in Holy triumph? Where was the Messiah who was going to right all wrongs? The Anointed One of God, the king of the Jews was peacefully surrendering to those who came to take Him away. The disciples did not understand what was happening before their very eyes.

For the faithful men who had been with Jesus at the time of his arrest, their hope was swiftly being marched away. Jesus would soon be standing before the Roman Governor Pilate. Matthew 27:11, *Meanwhile Jesus stood before the governor, and the governor asked him, "Are you the king of the Jews?" "Yes, it is as you say," Jesus replied*. Jesus was the king of the Jews. In fact, we are given in Revelation a panoramic description of king Jesus. *On his robe and on his thigh, he has this name written: KING OF KINGS AND LORD OF LORDS* (Revelation 19:16).

Pilate consider the charges against Jesus after hearing the answers Jesus gave Pilate to his questions, and concluded Jesus was an innocent man. John 18:36-38, [36] *Jesus said, "My kingdom is not of this world. If it were, my servants would fight to prevent my arrest by the Jews. But now my kingdom is from another place."* [37] *"You are a king, then!" said Pilate. Jesus answered, "You are right in saying I am a king. In fact, for this reason I was born, and for this I came into the world, to testify to the truth. Everyone on the side of truth listens to me." [38] "What is truth?" Pilate asked. With this he went out again to the Jews and said, "I find no basis for a charge against him. [39] But it is your custom for me to release to you one prisoner at the time of the Passover. Do you want me to release 'the king of the Jews'?"*

The hostile Jewish crowds that the hypocritical Jewish officials had stirred up was after Jesus so they told Pilate to release the criminal Barabbas instead of the innocent Jesus. John 19:1-7, *[1] Then Pilate took Jesus and had him flogged. [2] The soldiers twisted together a crown of thorns and put it on his head. They clothed him in a purple robe [3] and went up to him again and again, saying, "Hail, king of the Jews!" And they struck him in the face. [4] Once more Pilate came out and said to the Jews, "Look, I am bringing him out to you to let you know that I find no basis for a charge against him." [5] When Jesus came out wearing the crown of thorns and the purple robe, Pilate said to them, "Here is the man!" [6] As soon as the chief priests and their officials saw him, they shouted, "Crucify! Crucify!" But Pilate answered, "You take him and crucify him. As for me, I find no basis for a charge against him." [7] The Jews insisted, "We have a law, and according to that law he must die, because he claimed to be the Son of God."*

Jesus would be sentenced to death by crucifixion and soon the deed was done. The one Jesus faithful disciples had hoped to be the redeemer of Israel was now dead. Along with the death of Jesus, came the death of hope for many of His disciples. It is terrible to be at a place void of any hope. There are no more tragic words than "no hope."

Jesus' body was taken down from the cross and placed in a tomb. The Roman seal representing the power and authority of Rome was placed on the outside of the tomb. An elite guard of soldiers was assigned to stand guard around the clock to make sure no one would steal His body. This was an effort to stop any rumors of any possible claim of His resurrection.

No tomb, no seal, nothing in all creation could keep Jesus from resurrection. Romans chapter 1:4 speaks to the fact the Jesus "...was declared with power to be the Son of God by his resurrection from the dead: Jesus Christ our Lord." Resurrection power is a sign of Almighty power. The resurrection of Jesus proved He is the *KING OF KINGS AND LORD OF LORDS.*

Our Lord was lied about, but lies could not hold him down – He has risen! Our Lord was hated, but hate could not hold him down – He has risen! His opponents were jealous of him, but jealousy could not hold him down – He has risen! Jesus was persecuted, but persecution could not hold him down –   Jesus was slandered, but slander could not hold him down – He has risen! Jesus was crucified, but not even death, the grave, and all the powers of hell or the forces of darkness could hold him down – He has risen!

The resurrection of Jesus gave hope to the disciples who had lost hope. Resurrection changed the lives of the early disciples and should change our lives as well. Things do not always go the way we had planned. Some of the bigger obstacles in this life can be a serious illness, a tragedy, a relationship gone sour, marriage problems, job loss, or even the death of a loved one.

It is during these confusing and difficult times that we struggle to maintain hope until we remember the hope we have in Jesus. The hope we have in His resurrection power is available to us. Where there is real hope there is life. And where there is real life there is Jesus. Jesus is our hope now and for eternity.

When Jesus Christ was arrested prior to the cross many of His disciples put some distance between themselves and Jesus. Their hopes and dreams were buried with Jesus in the tomb. They were depleted and they needed to refuel. They were disillusioned. They were demoralized. They were depressed. They were defeated.

Jesus' disciples had an emptiness inside until the resurrection power showed up in the person of Jesus. John 20:19, *On the evening of that first day of the week, when the disciples were together, with the doors locked for fear of the Jews, Jesus came and stood among them and said, "Peace be with you!"* What happened in that room forever changed these men. Those who were once empty were now empowered by the resurrection power. Those who were once defeated, discouraged and demoralized were full of boldness because of resurrection power.

By His resurrection power Jesus filled them up with hope when they were running on empty. This same power is available to us today. Ephesians 3:20, *Now to him who is able to do immeasurably more than all we ask or imagine, according to his power that is at work within us.* God is able. God is able to do more than we can comprehend. And why is He able? He has resurrection power!

Find Hope in God's Power

God is able to do more for us than we can begin to comprehend. The creative Designer made the oceans, mountains, clusters of stars, and everything else we can read about in the first chapter of Genesis. Genesis 1:11-12, *[11] Then God said, "Let the land produce vegetation: seed-bearing plants and trees on the land that bear fruit with seed in it, according to their various kinds." And it was so. [12] The land produced vegetation: plants bearing seed according to their kinds and trees bearing fruit with seed in it according to their kinds. And God saw that it was good.*

His ultimate creative design came when He made man and woman and set them down in a garden paradise. Genesis chapter 2 offers one of the most significant images of God that we can ever capture. People have all kinds of inaccurate ideas about God and who He is. But one of the most important images we have to grasp is that God has always wanted a place, a special place, for those He has created in His image. God has always wanted to pour out His blessings on His people and there is no greater blessing than having His great power at work within us.

God is able to do more with our lives than we can imagine when His power is working in us. What can He do with our challenge, our weakness, our problem? He can do more, far more than we can imagine. God wants to give us the most important kind of power – His Power. God gives us His power to deal with our problems not because we deserve it, but because we have put our faith in the resurrected Lord. We can find hope in God's resurrection power.

CHAPTER 4 – QUESTIONS
TO DISCUSS, DEVELOP, AND DETERMINE

1. If a person is not fully convinced that Christ has all power, coupled with the desire to deliver them from Satan's pull, what will be the result?

2. What is one of the most amazing things about God's power? What can God's power do for us?

3. List three things that the resurrection can do for us. What is meant by the term "inner man" or "inner being" in Ephesians 3:16?

4. How does God refill our energy tanks? How does God fill us up when we are running on empty?

5. What must we do for God's resurrection power to be at work in our inner being? How does our spiritual appetite affect our hope or the power of God working in us?

6. Why did the disciples not understand Jesus' showing no resistance to His arrest by the soldiers? What did the arrest and later His crucifixion do to many of the Lord's disciples?

7. What did the resurrection do for the disciples who felt defeated and empty?

8. Explain some reasons why we should not be surprised that God is more than able to do more than we can imagine. What has God always wanted to do for His people?

FIND HOPE IN GOD'S PRECIOUS LOVE
(Ephesians 2:1-5, 3:17b-19)

Ephesians 2:1-5 reads, *¹ As for you, you were dead in your transgressions and sins, ² in which you used to live when you followed the ways of this world and of the ruler of the kingdom of the air, the spirit who is now at work in those who are disobedient. ³ All of us also lived among them at one time, gratifying the cravings of our sinful nature and following its desires and thoughts. Like the rest, we were by nature objects of wrath. ⁴ But because of his great love for us, God, who is rich in mercy, ⁵ made us alive with Christ even when we were dead in transgressions – it is by grace you have been saved.*

These verses from Ephesians have always been among my favorite passages in the entire Scripture. Ephesians 2:1-3 reveals a graphic description of our life without Christ, but fortunately the context does not stop there. The following verses give us insight into the heart of God and His passionate desire to pursue us with His great love. God's love instills hope in us. We can find hope in God's Word as it communicates His amazing love for us.

God's love surrounds us in our time of need. The psalmist understood the vital connection between our hope in God, God's love, and our redemption. He said, Psalm 130:7, *O Israel, put your hope in the LORD, for with the LORD is unfailing love and with him is full redemption.* Hope centered in God's love which brings redemption our way revives our hearts in times of trouble. *My soul faints with longing for your salvation, but I have put my hope in your word* (Psalm 119:81).

I have never literally fainted, but I have known a few people who have fainted. The fall may have been due to a stroke or some imbalance in their system. If we have seen someone faint, we would understand the person fainting did not realize they were fainting. We faint and then we fall down. The writer of Psalm 119:81 was not literally fainting, but he stated his soul was on the way down.

Life's pressures are real. Satan constantly works to distress and deplete our souls. God on the other hand is in the revival business. God wants to bring life into our lifelessness. He wants to restore, refresh, and redeem our souls. God's business can be summed up with the word love. The psalmist knew his only hope was in God's love and that unfailing love would uplift his soul.

Psalm 119:76, *May your unfailing love be my comfort, according to your promise to your servant.* When we catch even a glimpse of the unfailing makeup of God's love, we will not be surprised God's love comes to our rescue. Psalm 32:10b, *the LORD's unfailing love surrounds the man who trusts in him.* We can count on God's love, and it is in His love that we find hope. When we trust in God, we can be confident His love will surround us and comfort us.

The psalmist was in trouble and he requested God's help. Psalm 119:86, *All your commands are trustworthy; help me, for men persecute me without cause.* He begged God to help him in his trouble, and out of love God helped him. Hope based on

God's love for us will supply all the fuel we will ever need to feed our souls during times of trouble. Our hope is entrenched in God's amazing love. Against the darkness of our sins and miserable background of our spiritual failures appears a God who brings light, love, and mercy. God's love lights up our soul because His love is rich in mercy. When we hope in God's Word, we will find hope from His love. Psalm 119:88, *Preserve my life according to your love, and I will obey the statutes of your mouth.*

Psalm 94:17, *Unless the LORD had given me help, I would soon have dwelt in the silence of death.* When a person needs help, they need it immediately. The person needing help is not interested in a long speech. Someone drowning and going under for the last time does not have time to give an eloquent plea for assistance. The plea of the psalmist rings out the urgency – help me! He had come to the understanding that if God did not help Him, there was no one else who could provide hope. *Find rest, O my soul, in God alone; my hope comes from him* (Psalm 62:5).

Too often we place our hope in the wrong place and the wrong source. It is easy to get off track even for us followers of God. Trouble comes our way and we begin to place our hope in our job, our bank accounts, or our education. We may place our hope in some medical physician who is recognized for his expertise. It a blessing to have a good doctor when we face a serious health issue, but we must not forget to put our hope in the Great Physician of our soul.

While there is a benefit to our being optimistic in life's pressure cooker situations, we must never forget that Christian hope is more than being optimistic. We can have an expectant hope that God's love pursues us, surrounds us, and will sustain us in our times of trouble. Psalm 23:4, *Even though I walk through the valley of the shadow of death, I will fear no evil, for you are with me; your rod and your staff, they comfort me.* When we place our hope in God's Word, we obtain a hope that can endure any trouble.

The troubled psalmist was in desperate circumstances and to his credit he put his hope in the assurance of God's love. The palmist found hope in God's Word that communicated God's love for him in times of trouble. This is why he acknowledged that God could preserve or revive him by His love. Psalm 119:88, *Revive me according to Your lovingkindness, so that I may keep the testimony of Your mouth* (New American Standard Bible). The New American Standard Bible inserts the word "revive" in Psalm 119:88, while the New International Version uses the word "preserve." The idea behind these words is that God will invigorate our souls when they are on the verge of fainting.

When our souls need help, we can count on God's love coming to the rescue. Our responsibility in such times of trouble is to put our hope in God. Never doubt the desire God has in His heart to fill us full of His love. God's love revives and refreshes our souls with hope. When His love lives in us it makes all the difference in the world when we encounter problems. This is the hope-filled message that is repeated over and over in the Psalms.

Psalm 119:87, *They almost wiped me from the earth, but I have not forsaken your precepts.* Almost is a key word. His enemies, his problems "almost" wiped him from the earth, but he held on to his hope in God's love. What was the result? God's love revived his heart; God still revives hearts today. His precious love pursues us, and it is a marvelous theme imbedded in the heart of God.

God provides us an opportunity to experience the fullness of His love by being saved from our sins. The knowledge of our being in a saving relationship with God fills us with hope. The believers in the early verses of Ephesians 2 were reminded they used to follow the ways of the world. Paul said it this way, *in which you used to live when you followed the ways of this world and of the ruler of the kingdom of the air, the spirit who is now at work in those who are disobedient* (Ephesians 2:2).

The word "world" in Ephesians 2:2, speaks to following our will instead of God's will. Before these believers became Christians, there was a time when they were living, knowingly or unknowingly, according to the will of Satan. Satan does not care if we give him credit for our disobedience to God as long as we live worldly. To live worldly is to live only for what is temporary. The apostle referenced this idea of worldliness when he used the phrase, "Their mind is on earthly things" (Philippians 3:19).

The worldly crowd is bound to worldly things and worldly thoughts. The worldly mind has no room for God because it is saturated with only the thoughts and things of this world that have enslaved it to sin. The Ephesians had once lived solely on the worldly system. The New King James Version in Ephesians 2:3 reads, *among whom also we all once conducted ourselves in the lusts of our flesh, fulfilling the desires of the flesh and of the mind, and were by nature children of wrath, just as the others.* The result of this kind of living is to be dead in our sins. There are not varying degrees of spiritual deadness. To be dead in our sins is to be dead.

We should never forget what it was like to be under the wrath of God. To be under God's wrath is to be dead in our sins and headed for an eternity of suffering separated from God's love. To be under God's wrath is to be dead and headed to a place void of any hope at all. Thankfully, God's love called us out of our sin and shame. God's love called us out of the darkness and into the light. God's love reached out and pursued us by sending Jesus to this earth to be robed in human flesh so that we might one day be made alive with Christ.

There is no greater problem on this earth than the problem of sin. God the Father knew we could not make ourselves alive from sin. What did God do for us? He ushered into this world His precious love, embodied in the One called Jesus, and through His love extended to us an incredible hope of being saved. We cannot fully understand such love God has for His creation. God has always desired us to be with Him, freed from sin's condemnation, and surrounded by His love. In fact, God wants to fill us with His love, and with His love comes hope.

The Bible magnifies God's love for us in both the Old and New Testaments. God's love gives us hope to live beyond our problems and obstacles. His love continues to bring life to spiritually dead souls. Regardless of how depleted our soul may be, His mighty love will come to our rescue. Regardless of what we have done or left undone; we are not beyond being receivers of God's passionate love.

Love is the great hope of the Christian message. God offers hope for the hopeless, help for the helpless, and relief for our sin-sick soul. Remember, Ephesians was written to Christians, but they had not always been believers. The point is emphasized in no uncertain terms. *As for you, you were dead in your transgressions and sins* (Ephesians 2:1). Without God we are hopeless, helpless, and without life in our souls. This is why the powerful message of love rings out so loudly for us.

Ephesians 2:4-5, *But because of his great love for us, God, who is rich in mercy, ⁵ made us alive with Christ even when we were dead in transgressions – it is by grace you have been saved.* We will focus on God's provision of grace in the next chapter; here let us further examine the thrilling depth of God's love. Ephesians 3:17b-19, *¹⁷ᵇ And I pray that you, being rooted and established in love, ¹⁸ may have power, together with all the saints, to grasp how wide and long and high and deep is the love of Christ, ¹⁹ and to know this love that surpasses knowledge – that you may be filled to the measure of all the fullness of God.* What do these words do for our hope tank?

We have never owned a measuring tape long enough to be able to measure God's love for us. We have all kinds of technology that do incredible things. We have devices that will measure distances into the outer regions of space, but these measuring devices are unable to measure God's unlimited love. We cannot with our natural mind absorb such love. What we can do, and must do, is appreciate God's love.

God loves us beyond measure and that is why this love surpasses knowledge. There is an unusual love story in the Old

Testament that captures our imagination into God's limitless love for His people. The story stretches our minds and presents evidence that God's love for us is beyond our ability to measure. There is a love story woven through the minor prophet book of Hosea. It contains a message we would normally never associate with any normal, reasonable type of love.

God preserved the story of Hosea and Gomer to give us insight into His precious love. God tells His prophet Hosea to marry a woman, named Gomer, who is to say the least, unfaithful. Hosea 1:1-2, *¹ The word of the LORD that came to Hosea son of Beeri during the reigns of Uzziah, Jotham, Ahaz and Hezekiah, kings of Judah, and during the reign of Jeroboam son of Jehoash king of Israel: ² When the LORD began to speak through Hosea, the LORD said to him, "Go, take to yourself an adulterous wife and children of unfaithfulness, because the land is guilty of the vilest adultery in departing from the LORD."*

Even if we happen to be familiar with the story of Hosea, it is no less shocking to us. It seems unreasonable to us that God would tell his faithful prophet to marry a woman who was sure to be unfaithful. This is one of the most shocking love stories we could ever imagine. However, the story is representative of God's love for His people and the story does not stop with Hosea and Gomer. God opens the curtain of His love in the scriptures in many ways before and after the story we have in Hosea. Ultimately the story takes us to the Lord and Savior we read about in the New Testament, Jesus Christ.

We do not deserve God's love, which brings us back to Hosea's story. It is more than a love story about a marriage between Hosea and Gomer. Hosea unwraps the story of God and Israel and it sheds insight to our story as well. We find it troubling to imagine what it would be like to enter into a marriage with a woman like Gomer. Nonetheless, God directs Hosea to marry her. Hosea marries her even though he is sure he will experience an enormous amount of emotional pain directly from choosing to marry this woman.

This love story is not about a spouse who becomes unfaithful sometime down the road after the couple marry. This marriage partner was unfaithful from the very first day and anyone at the wedding would have known, based on her present actions, she would be disloyal to her husband. The suffering and the humiliation that Hosea willingly went through for his wife helps us better see and understand the depth of the love that fills the heart of God.

Gomer would disappear for days at a time. God directed Hosea to choose Gomer which was representative of God choosing Israel. Hosea committed his all to Gomer, but she was unfaithful. The resounding message from the book of Hosea is that God loves until it hurts and He keeps on loving through the pain of a repeatedly broken heart. To love and continue to love an unfaithful wife is an amazing kind of love.

We may naturally ask, "Why would Hosea marry Gomer?" The short answer of course, is that God told him to marry her. Hosea would be faithful to her regardless of her loose morality, embarrassing unfaithfulness to Hosea, and totally shameless activity open to public view. After careful reflection we should consider why in the world would God devote Himself to a people who in His foreknowledge knew would be disloyal to Him. God chose to love them is the short answer.

The short answer gets to the point, but His love is beyond our complete comprehension. No doubt God's love can bring us hope as we just attempt to grasp how wide, long, high, and deep is the love of God. The theme of God's love for His people woven through Hosea helps us see how God's love pursues us to the point we can no longer consciously deny His great love for us.

Gomer would disappear from Hosea's view for days at a times. He may or may not have known where she was, but he always knew she was up to no good. Eventually, Gomer's sin took her so far away from Hosea and had worn her out so completely that she would in essence be sold as a slave on an auction block. God then directed Hosea to do the unthinkable, and by carrying out this act of faithful love, he presented a dramatic picture of God's love for His adulterous people.

Hosea 3:1-3, [1] *The LORD said to me, "Go, show your love to your wife again, though she is loved by another and is an adulteress. Love her as the LORD loves the Israelites, though they turn to other gods and love the sacred raisin cakes." [2] So I bought her for fifteen shekels of silver and about a homer and a lethek of barley. [3] Then I told her, "You are to live with me many days; you must not be a prostitute or be intimate with any man, and I will live with you."*

Hosea's action toward his unfaithful and disgraced wife was a visible demonstration of the depth of God's love. God's love is longsuffering, but the love story has an attachment near this juncture in the book of Hosea. God brings a warning and a charge against His people in chapter 4. God's love has gone beyond a distance that can be measured with any measuring tool in His effort to get His people to come to their senses and return to His love.

Hosea 6:1-3, *¹ Come, let us return to the LORD. He has torn us to pieces but he will heal us; he has injured us but he will bind up our wounds. ² After two days he will revive us; on the third day he will restore us, that we may live in his presence. ³ Let us acknowledge the LORD; let us press on to acknowledge him. As surely as the sun rises, he will appear; he will come to us like the winter rains, like the spring rains that water the earth.* God's love will not end, but if we continue to reject His love when we have opportunity to receive the refreshing water of hope, He can bring to our souls, we will be sorry for eternity.

The people in Hosea's day had quit paying attention to God's Word. All through the Bible we can read how God tried various things to try to get the attention of His unfaithful people. God's people have a long history throughout the Scripture of turning their attention away from God's love. What did God do out of His love for His people in these times when they quit paying attention to His Word? What did He do when His people forsook Him? He used prophets to try to wake them up and reroute their attention.

The prophet Jeremiah for example exhorted Israel, who had moved away from worshipping God, to take an exam. Lamentations 3:39-40, *³⁹ Why should any living man complain when punished for his sins? ⁴⁰ Let us examine our ways and test them, and let us return to the LORD.* The psalmist even asks the Lord to examine him. Psalm 139:23-24, *²³ Search me, O God, and know my heart; test me and know my anxious thoughts. ²⁴*

See if there is any offensive way in me, and lead me in the way everlasting.

The Psalmist reflected on how God gave him a test to examine his heart. *Though you probe my heart and examine me at night, though you test me, you will find nothing; I have resolved that my mouth will not sin* (Psalm 17:3). God tests us for our own good. He wants to make sure we are paying attention and He knows when we are not. His love reaches out to us in order to try to wake us up when we are not where we ought to be.

God's love is far-reaching and wide-ranging, but it can be disregarded. His love can be ignored to the point that His wrath will be poured out on those who continue to rebel against Him by following the way of worldliness. There is a stern warning that surfaces in 1 Corinthians 10. The words of caution are directed to some believers in an effort to help them avoid the same disobedience of their forefathers. The apostle wrote, *¹ For I do not want you to be ignorant of the fact, brothers, that our forefathers were all under the cloud and that they all passed through the sea. ² They were all baptized into Moses in the cloud and in the sea. ³ They all ate the same spiritual food ⁴ and drank the same spiritual drink; for they drank from the spiritual rock that accompanied them, and that rock was Christ. ⁵ Nevertheless, God was not pleased with most of them; their bodies were scattered over the desert* (1 Corinthians 10:1-5).

The apostle emphasized that all the Israelites who left Egypt with Moses had seen God's mighty hand of love and power when God delivered them through the Red Sea. God's people lived to see that mighty miracle with their own eyes, but their faith did not remain strong. The Christians in Corinth were reminded of the seriousness to continue to honor God and to appreciate His love.

1 Corinthians 10:6, *Now these things occurred as examples to keep us from setting our hearts on evil things as they did.* What happened to those who snubbed God's love in the day of Moses has been written down as a warning for us (1 Corinthians 10:11). The Israelites of old not only made history, they made history that was recorded for us so we might not make the same mistakes. The warning is clear. 1 Corinthians 10:12, *So, if you think you are standing firm, be careful that you don't fall!*

God the Father instructs us in Proverbs 7:1-2, *¹ My son, keep my words and store up my commands within you. ² Keep my commands and you will live; guard my teachings as the apple of your eye.* Paying attention to God's Word is evidence that we love God and desire to please Him. Deuteronomy 7:12, *If you pay attention to these laws and are careful to follow them, then the LORD your God will keep his covenant of love with you, as he swore to your forefathers.*

The apostle went on to tell the believers in Corinth to test themselves. 2 Corinthians 13:5, *Examine yourselves to see whether you are in the faith; test yourselves. Do you not realize that Christ Jesus is in you – unless, of course, you fail the test?* God is not against testing us for our good and He is not against directing us to take our own test.

Tests help reveal what we know, what we believe, who we love, and what is going on inside us. When we get away from the Word of God we will suffer spiritually and if we are not careful, we might end up suffering for eternity. Satan actively tries to deceive us into thinking that God's love will always be there regardless of how long we reject His truth and dismiss His love. If we stay on the path of despising God's love, one day we are in for a rude awakening.

When Satan tempts us to feel comfortable in our relationship with God, when we should not feel comfortable because of our unrepented sin, we need an examination based on God's Word. There is great value in having regular spiritual checkups. Annual spiritual checkups are not sufficient. When we quit having regular checkups, we are going to find ourselves with heart trouble that no physical physician can repair.

There are all kinds of reasons for a physical doctor to schedule a physical test or an examination. The main reason for any test is to collect data and make assessments on what is or is not happening inside us. Our great Physician, God, knows where we are in our relationship with Him before He gives us a test. Because He loves us, He may test us or allow us to be tested so we may become more attentive to where we are putting our attention.

Spiritual examinations reveal where we are putting our focus. Are we putting our hope in His love or are we taking His enduring love for granted? We tend to take many of the blessings of God for granted. Unless we guard our hearts as the Proverb writer tells us in Proverbs 4:23, we will be prone to slip back into the ways of the world.

Satan tries to get us to take our blessings for granted. We are inclined to take for granted the spiritual blessing of love that

God has for us. When we are not giving God our full attention, we will even take our physical blessings for granted, including those blessings that He extends to us that sustain our lives. For example, people may take the rain and sunshine God sends their way for granted unless they happen to be the ones planting sections of corn, or cotton, or other valuable crops.

The people in Hosea's day became oblivious to God's love and the physical blessings He had provided. Hosea 2:8, *She has not acknowledged that I was the one who gave her the grain, the new wine and oil, who lavished on her the silver and gold – which they used for Baal*. Satan works to redirect our attention away from God's love. Unless we are careful and pay close attention, he will succeed.

We tend to take so many blessings for granted. It has been my observation we are prone to take the air and oxygen God gives us every minute of every day for granted until we are short of air and oxygen. My father and mother both spent the last days of their lives on machines connected to all sorts of tubes. These life support machines are mechanical ventilation machines. They are designed to help a patient breath when the person is too weak or ill to effectively breath. These machines are designed to be temporary and help a patient get over the hump of a difficult operation or a traumatic accident.

We need God's love as much as we need air. Actually, we need God's love more than we need air. Air will be of no use to us when our spirit leaves our physical body (James 2:26). Therefore, we must never be complacent in taking God's love for granted in our lives. His many blessings flow as regularly as the ocean waves roll to the shoreline. Psalm 147:11, *the LORD delights in those who fear him, who put their hope in his unfailing love.*

May we express our thanks to God for His love by giving Him continual thanks for the spiritual and physical blessings we enjoy. We may use a different selection of words and use different ways to express our thanks to God, but God wants to hear our hearts beating with the beat of thankfulness. For myself, I rarely go a day when I do not verbally communicate to God out loud by saying, "thank you." There are some hours of the day I may say those words multiple times. I am sure for every out loud "thank you" I have directed to God in my life, there are many more internal expressions of thanksgiving for His love.

When we are rooted in God's love (Ephesians 3:17b), we can be filled to the measure of all the fullness of God (Ephesians 3:19). What does it mean to be filled up to all the fullness of God? In one word it means we can have "hope." God's love fills our hearts with hope even though we do not deserve His unfailing love. In His wide-ranging love we find endless hope. 1 Corinthians 13:7, *It always protects, always trusts, always hopes, always perseveres.*

The people in Hosea's day needed to repent and return to God's extensive love. The same message is applicable in our day to anyone who needs to come home to God. God alone has a message of hope that initiates in His love for this sinful world. God's message of love came into focus when He sent the message of hope to Joseph, son of David, in Matthews 1:23, assuring him that God was at work. Matthew 1:23, *The virgin will be with child and will give birth to a son, and they will call him Immanuel – which means, "God with us."*

The hope Jesus represents today, as back then, is of no value to us unless we connect our ears, hearts, and feet to the message of hope – the hope represented in God's love by His sending Jesus to bring life to our dead souls. Let us not forget what is most important in this life as Satan seeks to sidetrack us. If we refuse to be distracted, disheartened, and deceived by the ways of this world, we will find hope in God's love.

CHAPTER 5 – QUESTIONS
TO DISCUSS, DEVELOP, AND DETERMINE

1. When our soul needs help what can we count on coming to our rescue? What did the psalmist ask God to do for him in Psalm 119:88?

2. What is our responsibility in times of trouble? What makes all the difference when we encounter a problem?

3. Explain what the Christians are reminded of in the early verses of Ephesians chapter 2.

4. What is it that Christians should never forget and why should we never forget this?

5. What is the great hope of the Christian message? Why is the story of Hosea and Gomer such a peculiar love story?

6. What is the resounding message we should get from Hosea? What were God's people not doing in Hosea's day? What did they need to do?

7. What mature thing did the psalmist do according to Psalm 139:23-24? Explain the purpose of the warning and cautionary words in 1 Corinthians 10:1-12.

8. What do spiritual examinations reveal? What do we have a tendency to do and how could we avoid this sinful trap? List three things we can refuse to do to find hope in God's love.

FIND HOPE IN GOD'S PROVISION
(Ephesians 2:6-10)

When I was around fifth grade my parents allowed me to start riding my bicycle to school. I liked it much better than riding the school bus for several reasons, but the main one was what I could do on the way home from school. My bicycle route took me through two vacant desert lots and around a sizable city park. On the way home I kept my eyes open for empty soda bottles. Those of us who are a bit older remember the time when most soft drinks were distributed in glass bottles.

The empty soda bottles were of interest to me because to a young boy it was like finding money on the street or along the path. In that day, soda bottles came with a refundable deposit attached to the price. It was an effort to get people to return the bottles so that they could be sterilized and used again. There would be times I would not even have to go out of my way to see an empty bottle.

My bicycle was perfectly equipped for the task. I had a stationary basket positioned between my handlebars and two side metal baskets that would hold a number of bottles in addition to my homework. I would collect the bottles during the week and on Saturday turn them in for candy at a little convenience store in the neighborhood. There would even be times on Saturday that I would purposely go hunting for more empty bottles.

All these years later I still recall the desire I had in my heart to just find one more, regardless of how many bottles I found that day. When I read the countless blessings of God in Ephesians, I recall my feeling on my soda bottle hunting trips of just wanting to find one more. We learn from Ephesians 1:3 that God has blessed us with *"every spiritual blessing in Christ."* God has graciously poured out His countless blessings upon His people. We should want to know every one of those blessings and fully experience them as we pursue our journey into a hope-filled life.

God provides us with blessings on top of blessings. We can find hope in God's provision; nowhere is this provision seen to be greater than in the blessing of His grace. God's heart of grace is the heart that is willing to extend repentant hearts one more. When we blow it and think there could not be any more grace in God's reservoir for us, God supplies what we need. How many times have we thought we have messed up too much, or too long, for God to pour any more grace in our direction? Yet, in our godly sorrow for our sin we look up in hope and find God willing to supply us one more dose of grace.

Ephesians 2:6-10, [6] *And God raised us up with Christ and seated us with him in the heavenly realms in Christ Jesus, [7] in order that in the coming ages he might show the incomparable riches of his grace, expressed in his kindness to us in Christ Jesus. [8] For it is by grace you have been saved, through faith – and this not from yourselves, it is the gift of God – [9] not by works, so that no one can boast. [10] For we are God's workmanship, created in Christ Jesus to do good works, which God prepared in advance for us to do.* The

Bible teaches salvation is a gift made available through our faith in Christ. We cannot earn our salvation or purchase it by merit on our part.

The spiritual victory we enjoy comes to us by God's provision of grace. It is grace that makes it possible for God to raise us up and seat us with Christ in the heavenly realms. Wow! What a hope builder to know that in spite of our sins there is hope. When we place our faith in Christ, repent of sin, and decide to follow Jesus, God provides us with grace. Grace fills us with a heavenly hope, regardless of our earthly troubles, because grace has saved us.

Grace has positioned us to enjoy the unparalleled riches of God. Grace provides us hope, and hope rooted in God's grace will get us from where we are to that place called heaven. God's grace moves us to a stronger resolve to be pleasing to God in all things. 1 Peter 1:13, [13] *Therefore, prepare your minds for action; be self-controlled; set your hope fully on the grace to be given you when Jesus Christ is revealed.*

One day our heavenly hope will see its fulfilment. Romans 6:5, *If we have been united with him like this in his death, we will certainly also be united with him in his resurrection.* There is a direct correlation between our salvation from sin and our being raised with Christ. The combination of our receiving grace and being raised with Christ exalts God's grace. Grace is God doing something for us we could never deserve.

No one gets to heaven without God's provision of grace. His provision of grace towards us when we cannot earn it or in any way deserve it, ushers hope into our hearts. If we foolishly think we could get to Heaven by earning our way, we are terribly wrong. No one will be saved any other way except by the grace of God.

The series of events leading up to Jesus' crucifixion were experienced firsthand by those close to Jesus. Jesus and His disciples came to Jerusalem to celebrate the Passover. Jesus was celebrated, betrayed, arrested, crucified, and then on third day He rose again. When Jesus was arrested in the Garden of Gethsemane shortly after the Last Supper, His disciples for the most part scattered.

All of the disciples, except Judas, were shocked by what was happening in front of their very eyes – Jesus was being taken away. Judas betrayed Jesus for thirty pieces of silver and then chose to take his own life in remorse for his sin. Judas shut down any chance of receiving God's grace. Judas did not understand the power of grace.

Peter in fear for his own life that night was quick to deny he even knew Jesus following His masters' arrest. Peter was afraid that what was happening to Jesus would happen to him.

Three times Peter denied He knew Jesus. Matthew 26:69-75, [69] *Now Peter was sitting out in the courtyard, and a servant girl came to him. "You also were with Jesus of Galilee," she said.* [70] *But he denied it before them all. "I don't know what you're talking about," he said.* [71] *Then he went out to the gateway, where another girl saw him and said to the people there, "This fellow was with Jesus of Nazareth."* [72]

He denied it again, with an oath: "I don't know the man!" [73]
*After a little while, those standing there went up to Peter
and said, "Surely you are one of them, for your accent gives
you away."* [74] *Then he began to call down curses on himself
and he swore to them, "I don't know the man!" Immediately
a rooster crowed.* [75] *Then Peter remembered the word Jesus
had spoken: "Before the rooster crows, you will disown me
three times." And he went outside and wept bitterly.*

Peter felt the crushing disappointment of his unfaithfulness
deep inside his heart. He was familiar with the words Jesus
had spoken earlier. Matthew 10:32-33, [32] *Whoever
acknowledges me before men, I will also acknowledge him
before my Father in heaven.* [33] *But whoever disowns me
before men, I will disown him before my Father in heaven.*
Peter knew he had denied Jesus at the moment Jesus may
have needed him the most.

All sins are repulsive, dreadful, and destructive, but to deny
Jesus and to go so far as to call a curse upon himself in his
denial of Jesus was incomprehensible. After Peter's third refusal
to admit he was a follower of Jesus, he went outside and wept
bitterly (Luke 22:62). The pain of sin is an all too common pain
for most of us. How do we come back from such sin? Grace.

We sin and we feel like it is all over. We see the words of
failure loop over and over on the screen of our minds. The
words of disappointment echo throughout our days and into
the nights – "We have blown it now!" We dwell on our sin and
we think there is no coming back from our sin. Satan will
definitely help us remember our sin, and then try and convince
us there is no hope for us now. God can never use us again.

We can all sympathize with what was probably running through Peter's mind after his three back-to-back denials. He had sinned before, and made plenty of sizable mistakes, but to deny he ever knew Jesus like he did was too much to comprehend. Peter quickly felt genuine remorse over his sin. He felt godly sorrow over the pain he caused God by his sin. Repentance unto God is a good thing, but without grace all of our sins would remain against us at judgment.

The angel dressed in white robe startled the women who came to the tomb early on the first day of the week. The women had planned to anoint the dead of body of Jesus, but He was no longer in the tomb. Mark 16:6-7, *⁶ "Don't be alarmed," he said. "You are looking for Jesus the Nazarene, who was crucified. He has risen! He is not here. See the place where they laid him. ⁷ But go, tell his disciples and Peter, 'He is going ahead of you into Galilee. There you will see him, just as he told you.'"*

Peter is given another opportunity to get it right. The angel told the women to go tell the disciples and Peter. I especially like the fact the angel mentioned Peter by name. I am sure that was no accident. Peter had so publicly denied Jesus that in Peter's shame he may have understandably felt there was no coming back from his sin. Peter had likely lost any hope of returning to the Lord. He must have thought his hope of being in heaven was gone forever. If Peter did think anything along these lines, he would have been decisively wrong.

Peter was called out among all the other disciples to be told His Lord was going ahead of him into Galilee. This news brought hope to Peter's ears. This is the Peter who would connect hope to God's grace. Peter would later say, *"set your hope fully on the grace to be given you when Jesus Christ is revealed."* Peter certainly did that himself. Peter experienced the grace of God in his life.

Peter found out what it means to be given another opportunity when he must have thought there were no more opportunities available. God is a God of another chance no matter what lie Satan tries to feed us. Peter later said, 1 Peter 5:8-9, [8] *Be self-controlled and alert. Your enemy the devil prowls around like a roaring lion looking for someone to devour.* [9] *Resist him, standing firm in the faith, because you know that your brothers throughout the world are undergoing the same kind of sufferings.*

Peter wanted to show his fellow Christians they could depend on God's grace through all kinds of sufferings and trials. 1 Peter 5:10, *And the God of all grace, who called you to his eternal glory in Christ, after you have suffered a little while, will himself restore you and make you strong, firm and steadfast.* He wanted those who have named the name of Christ to understand God's grace is all-sufficient. When we understand that God is in the restoring business, we find hope.

Christ himself will be active in restoring our souls in our time of need. God will restore, strengthen and support us so we can resist the devil and stand firm in the faith. These are hope-filled words that strengthen our resolve to resist giving in and giving up to Satan's evil influences. The enemy of our soul deliberately makes false accusations against God's people such as God is not going to give us another chance. We have blown our opportunities with God once and for all.

No matter what we are facing, God's grace will support us, strengthen us, and provide us with hope. When we find ourselves in the place Peter did and wonder if all hope is gone, we must remember the angel's words to the ladies at the tomb. Mark 16:7, "*But go, tell his disciples and Peter, 'He is going ahead of you into Galilee. There you will see him, just as he told you.'*" We can live with a sense of hope knowing we can be given a fresh start.

No matter how far we have fallen we are never too far down in sin to be washed cleaned by the blood of Christ and given a fresh start. Romans 4:7-8, *[7] Blessed are they whose transgressions are forgiven, whose sins are covered. [8] Blessed is the man whose sin the Lord will never count against him.* God does not put us at the back of the line like our elementary school teacher may have done when we messed up in class. We do not have to live in our failures; we can live in God's grace. Grace brings restoration our way.

Peter learned we can be restored from our sin and renewed to serve again by God's grace. The New Testament writers mention Peter's name over 200 times. In the four lists of apostles found in the New Testament, Peter's name is recorded first every time. Peter will later write out of his personal experience. *Cast all your anxiety on him because he cares for you* (1 Peter 5:7). It is great to be around people who care about us. There is benefit in our knowing people care and it encourages us. Yet, there is no greater encouragement than to know that in our struggles God cares. Because of God's provision of grace Peter becomes a prominent leader in the early church.

When we find ourselves in the place Peter did the night of his denials, we need to share his godly sorrow and step into God's provision of grace. All sinners need grace and all are sinners. Romans 3:23 states it clearly, *for all have sinned and fall short of the glory of God.* God has taken every measure imaginable to provide us with an opportunity for His grace. What we have to do to receive this gift of grace is to exhibit faith in God. Ephesians 2:8, *For it is by grace you have been saved, through faith – and this not from yourselves, it is the gift of God.*

The apostle Paul was careful to point out in Ephesians 2:9 our salvation is "not by works" and by this he means not by works of merit. Many have the mistaken idea that God has a set of eternal scales on which he balances our good works with our bad works and in the end, if the good outweighs the bad, we are escorted into heaven. If we believe that approach to salvation, we are guilty of believing the Devil's lie. More seriously, we will miss out on God's provision of grace that we need to be with Him in heaven.

It is God's provision of grace that brings us hope, not our good works. People all around us are walking around with the wrong benchmark of how we receive God's grace and are falling deeper and deeper into the hands of Satan's trap. Salvation is not something we buy, earn, or meritoriously achieve. It is a gift. Although it is gift, we still have to do some things. We have to love God, repent of our sins, confess Jesus as Lord, and be baptized into Christ as others did in the book of Acts. This is how those in the first-century became Christians.

Have we ever thought about this question, "How good is good enough?" If we do not have a proper view of grace and faith we may have wrestled with this question. The early verses of Acts 10 give us a good look at one man's life who was a very good man. His name was Cornelius. The biblical evidence we can compile from the Acts 10 and Acts 11 will help us answer the question, "How good, is good enough?"

Acts 10:1-8, *[1] At Caesarea there was a man named Cornelius, a centurion in what was known as the Italian Regiment. [2] He and all his family were devout and God-fearing; he gave generously to those in need and prayed to God regularly. [3] One day at about three in the afternoon he had a vision. He distinctly saw an angel of God, who came to him and said, "Cornelius!" [4] Cornelius stared at him in fear. "What is it, Lord?" he asked. The angel answered, "Your prayers and gifts to the poor have come up as a memorial offering before God. [5] Now send men to Joppa to bring back a man named Simon who is called Peter. [6] He is staying with Simon the tanner, whose house is by the sea." [7] When the angel who spoke to him had gone, Cornelius called two of his servants and a devout soldier who was one of his attendants. [8] He told them everything that had happened and sent them to Joppa.*

We can learn quite a bit about this man from Caesarea just by reading the first eight verses in Acts 10. Cornelius lived in Caesarea. Caesarea was a city deep Greek in culture and predominately populated by Gentiles. It was a city northwest of Jerusalem and there were some Jewish residents. Cornelius was a centurion of the Italian Regiment which meant he was an officer in the Roman army. A centurion was in charge of 100 men and his regiment was among the elite force of Rome.

Cornelius was a Gentile. Gentiles were outside of God's chosen people. The Jewish people were not allowed to associate with Gentiles. Later in the story Peter will say to Cornelius and others gathered in his house: *You are well aware that it is against our law for a Jew to associate with a Gentile or visit him. But God has shown me that I should not call any man impure or unclean* (Acts 10:28). Chronologically, it likely had been at least eight to ten years since the inception of the church we can read about in Acts 2. The Holy Spirit stepped in to guide the apostles into all truth as promised by Jesus (John 16:13).

At this juncture in the early church the Jewish Christians had not accepted any Gentiles into its fellowship. Cornelius was a devout man who feared God. He was deeply religious and believed in the God of Israel. He had converted to Judaism and to the God of Israel as some others Gentiles had done. Cornelius was a good man and was willing to help others – what a great characteristic for us to possess. Cornelius was a man who did not just pray about giving; we are told he gave generously. Someone may think he was saved because he gave generously to the needy, but that would be wrong.

Cornelius was a man who prayed to God regularly. Prayer is a defining mark of any follower of Jesus, but he was not saved because he was a man of prayer. Cornelius looks wonderfully good from our perspective; and he was a good man. Cornelius walked similar to a Christian, talked much like a Christian, prayed and gave generously as devoted Christians should, but all the good things we have noted thus far did not bring Cornelius into a saving relationship with God.

Granted, if we just stopped here Cornelius looks good enough to be saved; but we can never be good enough to merit God's grace. Cornelius would pass for a Christian in most people's eyes. He looked like a faithful Christian in that he prayed, feared God, was devout, and gave generously. Not only did Cornelius possess all these wonderful spiritual attributes, we learn a few more distinctively attractive things about him in the text.

We learn that Cornelius had an experience with an angel of God. His prayers were heard by God. He was obedient to the command God had spoken through the angel to send for the Apostle Peter. What an impressive resume this man had to his credit. If anyone could become a Christian and be saved by being a good man, Cornelius would have been that man. Cornelius sent two of his household servants along with a devout soldier to Joppa to get Peter.

As the events unfold from this point on in the story it helps us to determine whether or not Cornelius was a Christian and saved before he sent for Peter. We have to look at the rest of the story, which includes a vision Peter received to come to a biblical determination of whether Cornelius was saved before he heard God's message through Peter. As the men sent by Cornelius were approaching the city of Joppa the next day, Peter went up on his flat roof to pray. He was unaware that Cornelius had sent men to him. While on his roof Peter also had a vision.

God was going to have to convince Peter and the early church that God wanted Gentiles to be saved and become Christians. Peter, by way of a vision, was stretched into understanding that grace is available to Gentiles. Acts 10:9-13, *⁹ About noon the following day as they were on their journey and approaching the city, Peter went up on the roof to pray. ¹⁰ He became hungry and wanted something to eat, and while the meal was being prepared, he fell into a trance. ¹¹ He saw heaven opened and something like a large sheet being let down to earth by its four corners. ¹² It contained all kinds of four-footed animals, as well as reptiles of the earth and birds of the air. ¹³ Then a voice told him, "Get up, Peter. Kill and eat."*

It would be a difficult for Peter to explain his vision to the other apostles. He would have to do this eventually. Peter saw every kind of forbidden creature in the vision. The vision was pointing him to the grace that we all need. Peter in his vision did not just see a pig, he saw all kinds of four-legged animals. He likely saw things like camels, badgers, buzzards, bats, crocodiles, lizards, and all the things on the "don't eat" list found in Leviticus 11.

Acts 10:14-21, *¹⁴ "Surely not, Lord!" Peter replied. "I have never eaten anything impure or unclean." ¹⁵ The voice spoke to him a second time, "Do not call anything impure that God has made clean." ¹⁶ This happened three times, and immediately the sheet was taken back to heaven. ¹⁷ While*

Peter was wondering about the meaning of the vision, the men sent by Cornelius found out where Simon's house was and stopped at the gate. [18] They called out, asking if Simon who was known as Peter was staying there. [19] While Peter was still thinking about the vision, the Spirit said to him, "Simon, three men are looking for you. [20] So get up and go downstairs. Do not hesitate to go with them, for I have sent them." [21] Peter went down and said to the men, "I'm the one you're looking for. Why have you come?"

It was a lot for Peter, even as an apostle, to digest in a short span of time. The men who came from the house of Cornelius told Peter that Cornelius had a vision to send for him. Acts 10:22, [22] *The men replied, "We have come from Cornelius the centurion. He is a righteous and God-fearing man, who is respected by all the Jewish people. A holy angel told him to have you come to his house so that he could hear what you have to say."*

Peter invited the men into his house. The next day Peter along with some Jewish brothers from Joppa took off towards the house of Cornelius. When they arrived, Peter and the others with him entered the house of Cornelius. Cornelius had already gathered his relatives and close friends in anticipation of Peter's arrival. The story in Acts 10 is a reminder that even good religious people need to believe in Jesus and obey His message taught by the apostles.

Acts 10:25-35, [25] *As Peter entered the house, Cornelius met him and fell at his feet in reverence. [26] But Peter made him get up. "Stand up," he said, "I am only a man myself." [27]*

Talking with him, Peter went inside and found a large gathering of people. ²⁸ *He said to them: "You are well aware that it is against our law for a Jew to associate with a Gentile or visit him. But God has shown me that I should not call any man impure or unclean.* ²⁹ *So when I was sent for, I came without raising any objection. May I ask why you sent for me?"* ³⁰ *Cornelius answered: "Four days ago I was in my house praying at this hour, at three in the afternoon. Suddenly a man in shining clothes stood before me* ³¹ *and said, 'Cornelius, God has heard your prayer and remembered your gifts to the poor.* ³² *Send to Joppa for Simon who is called Peter. He is a guest in the home of Simon the tanner, who lives by the sea.'* ³³ *So I sent for you immediately, and it was good of you to come. Now we are all here in the presence of God to listen to everything the Lord has commanded you to tell us."*

Peter finally got God's point and confessed he understood the point of the vision. ³⁴ *Then Peter began to speak: "I now realize how true it is that God does not show favoritism* ³⁵ *but accepts men from every nation who fear him and do what is right"* (Acts 10:34-35). What Cornelius told Peter is helpful in drawing a verdict based on the Bible as to whether or not Cornelius was good enough to be saved by his prayers, his giving, and his angelic experience alone.

The story of Cornelius continues into Acts chapter 11 and we find some inspired insight there that helps us answer the question: "How good is good enough?" Peter was explaining his actions and his experience to the critics who had heard about his going into the house of Gentiles. Peter outlined his experience with the vision and the words spoken by the angel to himself and Cornelius. Acts 11:13-14, [13] *He [Cornelius] told us how he had seen an angel appear in his house and say, 'Send to Joppa for Simon who is called Peter.* [14] *He will bring you a message through which you and all your household will be saved.'*

If Cornelius needed to hear God's message from Peter about Jesus to be saved, then Cornelius could not have been saved prior to hearing it. God's Word indicates Cornelius and his household needed to hear how they could become receivers of the grace that saves. There is ample evidence from the Bible to arrive at this conclusion. Cornelius was an extremely good man, but he was not saved by the blood of Jesus prior to his hearing and accepting God's message of grace taught through Peter.

Cornelius put his faith in God's message delivered by Peter concerning Jesus' life, death, and resurrection. While Peter was speaking the message of hope-filled grace, the Holy Spirit came upon Cornelius and the others in an empowering way; and when they started speaking in tongues it only reinforced for Peter God's desire that Gentiles could be saved like the Jews. After seeing God's intervention Peter ordered that they *"be baptized in the name of Jesus Christ"* (Acts 10:48).

We cannot be good enough to be saved without hearing and accepting God's message of grace. We cannot offer up enough prayers or gifts to be saved without hearing and accepting God's message of grace. Regardless of our good works, prayers, and giving, we must also hear about the death, burial, and resurrection of Jesus and believe the message. This is where grace connects to every conversion story in the book of

Acts. Ephesians 2:8, *For it is by grace you have been saved, through faith – and this not from yourselves, it is the gift of God.*

When we place our faith in Jesus, repent of sin, and are baptized into the name of Jesus, we are showered with grace from above. We do not earn our salvation by believing, repenting, or being baptized. Our faith in God's Word brings us into contact with God's provision of grace, but in no way do we earn or deserve grace. Grace is the gift of God that saves and brings us hope.

The result of setting our hope fully on the grace of God is living with an appreciation of God's grace. 1 Peter 1:14, *As obedient children, do not conform to the evil desires you had when you lived in ignorance.* How could we not live differently after being touched by the amazing grace of God. 1 John 2:3-4, *[3] We know that we have come to know him if we obey his commands. [4] The man who says, "I know him," but does not do what he commands is a liar, and the truth is not in him.*

Faith moves us to obey God's commands and the idea of faith moving us in God's direction is the thread that runs through the entire Bible. Hebrews 11 verifies the importance of faith in the lives of God's faithful. When Peter received another chance to obey God by His extending grace to him, he did not abuse that grace. He served the Lord faithfully the rest his days on earth.

Our God is a God of more second chances than we will ever need. When we think of the story of Jonah and the big fish that God sent His way to swallow him, the fish was sent by the

God who was going to give Jonah another chance. We can know that because the fish did not eat Jonah, but housed him for a few days. Jonah 1:17, *But the LORD provided a great fish to swallow Jonah, and Jonah was inside the fish three days and three nights.*

God provided an opportunity for Jonah to repent and obey after he chose to disobey God. God had told Jonah to go to the city of Nineveh and preach to the wicked people. Jonah chose not to go to Nineveh, and of course, that was the wrong choice. Jonah would soon realize just how wrong it was not to obey God in the first place. Instead of going to Nineveh, Jonah headed for Tarshish by way of a ship. He paid his fare and thought he was on his way to Tarshish; for a while, he was headed to Tarshish. We will never be able to successfully run away from God. Jonah's story is proof of that fact.

God sent a great wind on the sea and the ship Jonah was on found itself in danger of breaking into pieces. The sailors feared for their lives and cast their cargo over into the sea trying to lighten the ship. The captain learned that Jonah was the one who was responsible for the storm they were encountering, and Jonah admitted he was the reason they were in trouble. Jonah made an unusual request in the midst of his disobedience. Jonah 1:12, *"Pick me up and throw me into the sea," he replied, "and it will become calm. I know that it is my fault that this great storm has come upon you."*

They reluctantly cast him overboard when all else failed, and the sea became calm. What did the LORD do? He provided a great fish. God is so gracious to us and it was no different for Jonah. God provided a fish to swallow Jonah, but not to eat Jonah. When Jonah's sin, stubbornness and rejection of God's Word caused him to be thrown overboard and to be in danger of drowning, the Lord provided for him. If it had not been for the big fish, he would have drowned.

We may have a similar story minus the big fish. When we were running away in disobedience to God, God did not give up easily on us. When we were in danger of spiritually drowning, the Lord gave us another chance. If we try to run from God, we are likely to end up where we never planned to be. When Jonah started out that day, he would never have thought this is the day I will be rolling around in the cesspool of a fish belly.

If we run from obeying God, He is willing to do whatever He can to try to get us to turn back to Him. He graciously gives us another chance to get right with Him. God went to great lengths to encourage Jonah to refocus his priorities. I think most people would choose to repent if they found themselves slipping and sliding around in the digestive cesspool of a fish's stomach for three days like Jonah.

Jonah had three days to think about his disobedience, but I would suspect those days seemed much longer. Jonah replaced his pride with prayer from inside the fish and to no surprise to us, God was gracious again. He made a clarifying statement in Jonah 2:9b, *Salvation comes from the Lord*. God spoke to the fish and the fish literally threw him up onto dry land (Jonah 2:10). God rescued Jonah from his sea of sin. Unfortunately, Jonah did not continue to live in appreciation of God's provision of grace.

The point of Jonah's story, Peter's story, and our story, is there is hope when everything looks hopeless. When we understand that we cannot be good enough to ever earn God's grace or the gift of salvation, we should always be thanking God for His grace. May we always seek to obey God and thank Him for providing a way out of our sin problems. While we cannot work to merit our salvation, God does expect us to work (Ephesians 2:10). As we work for the Lord in light of God's gift to us, we find hope in the abundance of His grace.

CHAPTER 6 – QUESTIONS
TO DISCUSS, DEVELOP, AND DETERMINE

1. What is the provision of God that allows us to get to heaven? What does Satan try to convince us of after we have sinned and blown it in God's sight?

2. What was Peter trying to get across to his fellow Christians by his words in 1 Peter 5:10? How does God's involvement in restoring us fill us with hope?

3. Describe who the blessed man is according to Romans 4:7-8.

4. Why did Peter weep bitterly after his denials of knowing Jesus? What did Peter's weeping over his sins demonstrate to God?

5. How did God encourage Peter by the words spoken to the ladies at the empty tomb? Explain how the words of 1 Peter 5:7 can encourage us.

6. Name some things we can know about Cornelius. What does the intersecting stories of Cornelius and Peter tell us about salvation? What did Cornelius understand that Peter would bring him?

7. Explain why Jonah's refusal at first to go to Nineveh proved to be a fatal choice. What did God provide for Jonah according to the Scripture, and what does this say about God?

8. What is the primary point from Jonah's story, Peter's story, and our story?

FIND HOPE IN GOD'S PROMISE

(Ephesians 2:11-3:6)

My memory challenges me at times. I wrote two words on a small piece of paper one day and stuck it to the area of my desk that collects notes. Most of my notes make it to my pocket calendar. This one did not because apparently when I wrote down the time and the date, I thought to myself there is no reason to write anything more than this brief information because there is no way I would forget what this upcoming date and time means. I did forget and my memory could not make any connection to the time and date.

This forgetfulness happened soon after I was hired to preach for a congregation. Thinking I may have promised to meet someone or do something for someone that because of my forgetfulness I was not going to do presented me a problem. I mentioned my predicament at the beginning of my next scheduled Bible class in hope it would trigger my memory. I mentioned to those in the class how I only put a date and a time on a note and confessed my memory had slipped me. I asked if the upcoming date and time I scribbled down had anything to do with them to please tell me after class.

I went on to tell those in the class that day, including the church leadership that had hired me, "At this point you may be thinking one of two things, why did we hire this guy, or I am happy to learn he is just like us." We all know the blessing of memory. When my mother passed away, I chose to do her memorial service. I understand why a preacher, or any family member, might choose not to do their loved one's memorial celebration. However, for me I could not imagine anyone else conducting her service.

There are many precious memories that flood our minds in such times of the death of a loved one or a close friend. There was no exception for me as my mind was running over with various memories. Some things end with death, but our precious memories do not. The good times, the good deeds, and the good words all continue to linger in our hearts and minds in these transition times of life. Those we love leave a legacy of memories that continues to shine bright in the lives of those they leave behind.

We make a promise and intend to keep the promise we make. There are times when we make a promise that we are unable to keep due to our health issue, or financial obligations, or any countless other things that can interfere with our keeping the promise we had planned to keep. We can add to that the reality that sometimes we may even forget the very promise we made until we are later called out about it. There are times we unintentionally forget and break our promises.

When God makes a promise to us, He never forgets and He always keeps His promises. Nothing ever gets in the way of God keeping His promises. The weather, the storms, and all the forces of evil at war in the spiritual realm cannot derail God from keeping the promises He has made to us. May we never forget our God is a promise keeping, promise blessing, and promise spreading God.

It is easy to forget certain things and perhaps that is why we find so many reminders in the Scripture. God's Word tells us over and over to remember our blessings and God's promises. Ephesians 2:11-3:6, continues to magnify our blessings and call to memory a particular promise. *[11] Therefore, remember that formerly you who are Gentiles by birth and called "uncircumcised" by those who call themselves "the circumcision" (that done in the body by the hands of men) – [12] remember that at that time you were separate from Christ, excluded from citizenship in Israel and foreigners to the covenants of the promise, without hope and without God in the world* (Ephesians 2:11-12).

The term "uncircumcised" in Ephesians 2:11, was a designation among the common Jews to point out the Gentiles were separated from a relationship with God and His many blessings. The term "Gentile" refers to anyone who is not Jewish. Among the other words that stand out in Ephesians 2:12, are the words "without hope" and "without God." Without hope means Gentiles had no hope. Their having no hope at one time was the consequence of not having God in their lives. God's blessings or promises were at one time unavailable to the Gentiles.

We are called to remember life without God. Israel was a nation under God with certain rights and privileges. Jews, as citizens of God, had tremendous blessings. God's protection and guidance was with the Jews, and the Gentiles were separated from being recognized as citizens of God. The apostle says, do not forget the time when you were without citizenship and *"foreigners to the covenants of promise."*

God's promises were directed to Abraham and his seed and not to the Gentile nations. God's covenant blessings were tied to the Jews through Abraham in Genesis 12:1–3. The exhortation in Ephesians is to "remember" the time when we had no hope, no God, and were separated from Christ. Remember the time when Gentiles had no life or fellowship with God. We must not forget what it was like, for when we forget we are most vulnerable to Satan's attacks.

Prior to the Gentiles' coming to Christ they were unconnected to the covenants and the promise made to Abraham. The Gentiles who sought to follow the God of the Jews were restricted from entering beyond the court of the Gentiles and could never enter the temple. They did not have the right of citizenship or family privileges in God's family. In the pagan city of Ephesus there were idols everywhere, but as the Gentiles worshipped these idols, they offered no hope to the worshipers. They could offer them no hope of citizenship in heaven. There was a time when the Gentiles were without the blessings reserved for the Jews.

In a few Jewish circles in the first century a Gentile might be able to convert to Judaism, but they were still not Jews. The English Standard Version reads, *Woe to you, scribes and Pharisees, hypocrites! For you travel across sea and land to make a single proselyte, and when he becomes a proselyte, you make him twice as much a child of hell as yourselves* (Matthew 23:15).

The Gentiles who sought the God of the Jews were known as "proselytes." The Greek word PROSELYTE in Matthew 23:15 in some Bible translations is translated "proselyte." Other translations like the New International Version translate the Greek word with the English word "convert." The New Testament refers to such a convert to Judaism as a "God-fearer," as was in the case of Cornelius. Rabbis often had a strong distaste for these converts; therefore, they never attained an equality with the Jews who worshipped in the synagogue.

It would be understandable because of the Jewish history that Jewish Christians would have great difficulty in comprehending the blood of Christ changed the separating lines for the Gentiles. This misunderstanding contributed to the reason God had to miraculously work a vision for the Apostle Peter in Acts 10 to get him to understand God's intent under the New Covenant for Gentiles (Acts 10:34-35). God wanted Gentiles to be incorporated into His forever family. The time has come where we can have hope, fellowship with God, and be members in God's household.

I checked five Bible translations I typically study from each week and in all five of them I noted Ephesians 2:13, begins with the same two words, "But now." These two words show the stark contrast of things we should remember. There is a significant contrast between the time of no hope and the time of now hope. "But now" in this context, are sweet sounding words to people who put their faith in Christ.

Ephesians 2:13-22, *[13] But now in Christ Jesus you who once were far away have been brought near through the blood of Christ. [14] For he himself is our peace, who has made the two one and has destroyed the barrier, the dividing wall of hostility, [15] by abolishing in his flesh the law with its commandments and* *regulations. His purpose was to create in himself one new man out of the two, thus making peace, ¹⁶ and in this one body to reconcile both of them to God through the cross, by which he put to death their hostility. ¹⁷ He came and preached peace to you who were far away and peace to those who were near. ¹⁸ For through him we both have access to the Father by one Spirit. ¹⁹ Consequently, you are no longer foreigners and aliens, but fellow citizens with God's people and members of God's household, ²⁰ built on the foundation of the apostles and prophets, with Christ Jesus himself as the chief cornerstone. ²¹ In him the whole building is joined together and rises to become a holy temple in the Lord. ²² And in him you too are being built together to become a dwelling in which God lives by his Spirit.*

Gentiles now have full access to all of God's blessings and promises. When Peter revealed inspired words of how we can become Christians in Acts 2 he was speaking only to Jews. Jews who had gathered for the Pentecost celebration celebrated once a year with the Jews in Jerusalem. The message God gave Peter was not to be limited to the Jews, but God would have to guide His apostles and the early church into that truth.

It would be somewhat natural for the apostles and the Jews in the first century to think only in terms of God's blessings for the Jews. They could not grasp the blessing of forgiveness and the promised Holy Spirit in Acts 2:38, could include the Gentiles. Evidence of that is seen in the lack of reaching out to the Gentiles with the gospel. When Peter declared in Acts 2:39, *The promise is for you and your children and for all who are far off – for all whom the Lord our God will call*, he was not even considering the far off being the Gentile population. The far off in his mind at this point were those Jews who were unable to come to Jerusalem for Pentecost.

We must not forget what it was like to be without heavenly blessings. When we fail to remember what it was like to be lost, Satan has us where he wants us. When we forget our spiritual blessings, we will simultaneously demonstrate a lack of appreciation for God. Psalm 103:2, *Praise the LORD, O my soul, and forget not all his benefits*. May we never forget the source of all our blessings because if we do, we will find ourselves once again being without hope and without God.

We can find hope in God's promise. Romans 4:16, *Therefore, the promise comes by faith, so that it may be by grace and may be guaranteed to all Abraham's offspring – not only to those who are of the law but also to those who are of the faith of Abraham. He is the father of us all.* Galatians 3:13-14, [13] *Christ redeemed us from the curse of the law by becoming a curse for us, for it is written: "Cursed is everyone who is hung on a tree."* [14] *He redeemed us in order that the blessing given to Abraham might come to the Gentiles through Christ Jesus, so that by faith we might receive the promise of the Spirit.* Galatians 3:29, *If you belong to Christ, then you are Abraham's seed, and heirs according to the promise.*

The time has come when God has brought together Jew and Gentile into one body. Ephesians 2:14 states that Jesus has *"destroyed the barrier, the dividing wall of hostility."* It may be hard for us to relate to the wall or partition that separated Jew and Gentile in the first century world, but it is not difficult to understand how walls, physical or imaginary, separate people from one another. Walls separate nations, communities, and families.

God delights in tearing down dividing walls of aggression and resentment through the blood of Jesus. God delights in healing broken marriages, broken families, and broken lives. God delights in bringing peace, but the peace He brings is only found in Christ. Jesus is our peace according to Ephesians 2:14. It is only His peace that can eliminate the hatred, prejudice, and other evils that take up residence in our hearts.

Jesus alone allows us to be at peace with God. Through Jesus, Jews and Gentiles have access to God the Father (Ephesians 2:18). No language barrier, no social-economic barrier, or anything else can keep us from being in God's faith family enjoying His blessings. 1 Corinthians 12:27, *Now you are the body of Christ, and each one of you is a part of it*. We can be united together in the body of Christ.

Jesus gives us life with Him and with one another in the body of Christ. Our commonality as Christians is ingrained in the fact that we all need Jesus and we share in the love of Jesus. We are different from each other, but still part of each other because we have the same cleansing blood that washes away our sins. God has brought us near to Him and made us citizens without distinction from one another. We are *"fellow citizens with God's people and members of God's household."* What does this mean? It means we are no longer separated from God or the special privileges that at one time were limited only to the Jews.

The fulfillment of God's promise is we can be one and members together in His family. This was the same message taught throughout the New Testament. Colossians 1:19-22, [19] *For God was pleased to have all his fullness dwell in him,* [20] *and through him to reconcile to himself all things, whether things on earth or things in heaven, by making peace through his blood, shed on the cross. [21] Once you were alienated from God and were enemies in your minds because of your evil behavior. [22] But now he has reconciled you by Christ's physical body through death to present you holy in his sight, without blemish and free from accusation.*

What does it mean to be reconciled? In simplest terms it means we are brought together. That which at one time alienated us from God and one another is no longer standing in the way of our fellowship. Reconciliation is at the center of our relationship with God and it is central to our being able to have hope. The cross from which Jesus' sinless blood flowed made reconciliation possible.

The Creator God we love, adore, and worship loved us His sinful creation so much that while we were still trapped in sin without any hope of solving our sin problem, or perhaps even recognizing it, sent His only begotten Son to pay the price for our sin. Jesus paid the price to set us free from the bondage of sin and death. The biblical writers are constantly trying to get across the value of our focusing on God's promises and the length He has gone to bless us.

By focusing on the promises and remembering the before and after reconciliation picture, our hearts will overflow with hope. When my mother passed away, I sat down and went through the stacks of pictures she had handed down to me. They brought back some comforting memories. Of course, the cameras in her day, or even when I was a child, were much different than what we have in the present day. I could not have imagined when we were children to one day have digital cameras or get our minds around cell phones that had the capability to take amazing pictures and to be able to send them across the country with a touch of a button.

As I looked through the old pictures of my mother and her family, one thing caught my attention. It was not that something new had been photoshopped into these old pictures because what I saw had been there all the time. Only with the passing of my mother I looked at the pictures more intently than I had probably done before. The thing that stood out to me in viewing the worn, torn, and crinkled photos of her family was that no one seems to be smiling in the pictures.

As I recall my mother taking pictures of my sister and me, she would encourage us to smile for the camera. We had to at least try to smile or say "cheese" before she snapped the picture button. Some of us adults have been known to make all kinds of goofy looking faces to try to get our own children or grandchildren to smile as we are taking a picture. When my mother was a child and definitely when her mother was a child, they must have taken a completely different approach to the way we take pictures today. And I am speaking to more than just the improved technology.

The picture takers in that period of history apparently had a much different approach to their picture taking than we do today. I mention these old pictures of my mother that brought me some wonderful memories to point out something I found a bit fascinating. Nearly every person captured in the picture displayed a somber, serious looking facial expression. I do not want to read too much into these expressions, but what kind of expression do you think God would expect to see on our face if He were to take a picture of us?

What would come to God's mind based on what He could see on our faces? Would He see people filled with smiles of hope and thankfulness? God deserves and expects to see our appreciation not only by way of our facial expressions, but by the words we choose to use each and every day. We should remember, God sees beyond our facial expressions, even beyond the words we speak. He sees what is going on inside our hearts. We are not the only ones that value the importance of remembering – God does as well.

The Ephesians writer emphasizes the value of our remembering and focusing on God's promises. We are no longer outside of the covenant promises of God and this provides us an anchor for our soul. Hope is an anchor that is unwavering and can withstand the spiritual winds of evil. The hope we have in Christ is a hope based on faith and not sight.

Hebrews 6:18 tells us *"it is impossible for God to lie"* and then the writer directs us to be encouraged and take hold of the hope God offers. *We have this hope as an anchor for the soul, firm and secure* (Hebrews 6:19a). There is nothing like an anchor in times of a storm. Hope helps anchor our souls. Jesus came to give us the great hope. We have the hope of peace, the guarantee of heaven, and the assurance of being sharers together in the promise in Christ.

God has joined us together in the church as He had previously promised and has now made what was once unknown, known by way of revelation to his apostle. Ephesians 3:1-6, [1] *For this reason I, Paul, the prisoner of Christ Jesus for the sake of you Gentiles –* [2] *Surely you have heard about the administration of God's grace that was given to me for you,* [3] *that is, the mystery made known to me by revelation, as I have already written briefly.* [4] *In reading this, then, you will be able to understand my insight into the mystery of Christ,* [5] *which was not made known to men in other generations as it has now been revealed by the Spirit to God's holy apostles and prophets.* [6] *This mystery is that through the gospel the Gentiles are heirs together with Israel, members together of one body, and sharers together in the promise in Christ Jesus.*

Five times between Ephesians 2:21-3:6 we find the word "together" (New International Version). God's mystery made known was that God brings people together. *Gentiles are heirs together with Israel, members together of one body, and sharers together in the promise in Christ Jesus.* These statements in Ephesians 3:6, make up the primary points in the concluding verses of Ephesians chapter 2. The same theme is spelled out in a precise, practical way in the early verses of chapter 3.

Since it is God's will to bring people together, the objective of the evil powers of darkness is to divide and destroy. We can be one and be right with God in spite of the evil forces of darkness. We can be members together in God's blood-bought church regardless of what has divided us in the past. Our commonality in the church, the one body of Christ, is rooted in the fact we all need Jesus and we are loved by Jesus. The result of God's love has made what was once impossible, possible – sinless blood has brought us near to God and to one another.

May we always remember the power of Jesus' sinless blood, for in it we find hope, and our hope in Christ is the anchor of our souls. Remembering our need for God and His many promises, and the particular promise that brings us peace must never escape our minds. When we were without hope and without God, God gave us hope and the assurance He is now with us never to leave us alone. We can remember His promise and all the other promises. As we remember our blessings attached to the promise of togetherness, revealed by the Spirit through the apostles, our hearts smile because we enjoy an enduring precious hope.

The word "hope" occurs around 75 times in the New Testament. If we were to look up those passages on hope we would discover hope is always connected in some way to God. I have noticed that there are some streets across the country that bear the name "Hope Street." It would be nice to live on a street called "Hope." We may never own a house on Hope Street, but we can live with hope every day.

1 Peter 1:3, *Praise be to the God and Father of our Lord Jesus Christ! In his great mercy he has given us new birth into a living hope through the resurrection of Jesus Christ from the dead.* What we need is the living hope found in Jesus; hope that is grounded on the promises of God. The promises of God motivate us when we understand that the Almighty Creator of the universe has made treasured promises to us. God has communicated precious promises which through Christ brings us hope.

2 Peter 1:4, *Through these he has given us his very great and precious promises, so that through them you may participate in*

the divine nature and escape the corruption in the world caused by evil desires. If we will stand on the promises of God, we will have hope, and hope will make a positive difference in the way we live our lives. The precious promises God has given us paves the way for us to participate in God's nature and escape the world's corruption.

At one time we were without hope and subject to the world's corruption. But when we placed our trust in Jesus we have hope regardless of where we physically live. We have a life-giving and a life-living hope that we can live with in our homes and at our places of employment. The hope we have as Christians will never fail because God is the source of our hope.

2 Timothy 1:1, *Paul, an apostle of Christ Jesus by the will of God, according to the promise of life that is in Christ Jesus.* Our hope comes from the hope of eternal life we have in the promise of Christ. God is trustworthy, reliable and absolutely faithful to every promise He makes. God's promises are not vague intangible ideas. His promise of life in Christ helps us to handle any challenge and gain a new outlook on what is most important in life – the promise of life.

The more we understand His promises, rely on them, and act on them the more hope-filled our lives will be. Hope in the promises of God can make a difference in our lives, our thoughts, our actions, and even our decisions, as we resolve to follow Jesus all the way to heaven. If we ever find ourselves on the way to the placed called discouragement, it is likely we have forgotten that at one time we were without hope. But now we have hope! Refocus, remember, and take hold of the hope of God's promise of life in Christ.

CHAPTER 7 – QUESTIONS
TO DISCUSS, DEVELOP, AND DETERMINE

1. What is noteworthy about God making promises to us?

2. Name several specific things Gentiles were told to remember. How does remembering these things help bolster our confidence to live hope-filled lives?

3. What does it mean in practical terms to be *"fellow citizens with God's people and members of God's household?"*

4. Explain what Peter was likely thinking in Acts 2:39 when he stated, *the promise is for you and your children and for all who are far off – for all whom the Lord our God will call.* What is the fulfillment of God's promise in the context of Ephesians 2:11-3:6?

5. What does it mean to be reconciled? What is the objective of the evil powers of darkness in light of God's objective?

6. What is the one thing we can know God will never do because He is unable to do it?

7. Approximately how many times is the word "hope" found in the New Testament?

8. What two things will the precious promises of God do for us? What can help us if we think we are on the way to the place called "discouragement?"

Chapter 8

FIND HOPE IN GOD'S PURPOSE
(Ephesians 3:7-13)

He was a song leader in the congregation where I was serving the Lord. We developed a special relationship, but I did not know what to think about him at first. I had been preaching in the congregation for just a few weeks. The fourth week after I finished my lesson, he came up to me and wanted to talk. He expressed his concern over my lessons, not the content of them, but their length. He expressed his concern to me as gently as he knew how.

He reminded me that the first week I preached a lesson that was only twenty minutes long. The second week I preached twenty-two minutes. The third week twenty-five minutes and my lesson that Sunday was twenty-seven minutes long. My concerned song leader said something like this to me, "If you keep this pattern up of adding a few minutes to your lesson each week, there will soon be people outside holding 'Free the Hostages' signs." He wanted to advise me on this potential problem. At the time I did not know just how to take his concern.

About two years later my song leader friend came up to me and said, "Clark, you know you are in trouble when your doctor informs you, 'This was not showing up the last time I examined you.'" The words came to the ears of my friend as he was getting his report from his routine yearly physical. His doctor had discovered on the preliminary tests what

136

appeared to be a mass in his abdomen. My friend could tell by the expression on his doctors face it was not good news!

His doctor was sure they needed further tests. He soon had a CAT scan and an MRI and was stuck with needles until finally it all boiled down to waiting for the results. He had to wait five to seven days to get any results. Perhaps we have found ourselves in a similar place, or having to wait for a loved one's report to come in from a medical specialist. Five days or more we wait and while we are waiting, we may know all too well that the dreaded "C" word, cancer, has a way of expanding the number of minutes into sleepless hours.

Five days when we are waiting for the results of such tests seem like months. When he was able to meet with his doctor about his test results, he learned he had stomach cancer. There is nothing good about the "C" word. His cancer was in the most advanced stage and it was a lot to absorb since he had not really had any overly noticeable symptoms up to this point. The lack of pain and discomfort he had experienced would soon change. Within a few months he would only be able to eat standing up and not much food in-take even in that position.

My friend was not only a good song leader, he was a good man. He loved God and cared about people, but he confessed to me something I would never have known unless he told me. He told me the test results had awakened him to eternity. Looking back on his life prior to the doctor finding the mass, he had taken life for granted in many areas. He had taken much for granted and in some ways, we could say he had just been coasting through life, even in his spiritual life.

He was a Christian, but he had been going through the motions and just kind of getting by in life. Life had become just a routine he explained until his medical exam found anything but routine. We have a tendency to live life without plugging into God's purpose, and not even realize it until a crisis or tragedy hits us. The "C" word, or some other serious health issue, appears out of nowhere and we take a firm look at our lives. It is like we take breathing and our regular routines for granted and life slips by us with no real thought of what is the purpose God has given us in life. What is life all about?

My friend enjoyed leading singing and fellow-shipping with other Christians, but he had missed something of God's purpose in his own life. Life for him had become somewhat automatic and disconnected to God's purpose for us in the church. My song leading friend had programmed his days without the purpose God places upon His people in the church. He had failed to partner with God to sound forth the good news of Jesus beyond the walls of the church assembly.

Ephesians 3:7-13, *7 I became a servant of this gospel by the gift of God's grace given me through the working of his power. 8 Although I am less than the least of all God's people, this grace was given me: to preach to the Gentiles the unsearchable riches of Christ, 9 and to make plain to everyone the administration of this mystery, which for ages past was kept hidden in God, who created all things. 10 His intent was that now, through the church, the manifold wisdom of God should be made known to the rulers and authorities in the heavenly realms, [11] according to his eternal purpose which he accomplished in Christ Jesus our Lord. [12] In him and through faith in him we may approach God with freedom and confidence. [13] I ask you, therefore, not to be discouraged because of my sufferings for you, which are your glory.*

God's purpose for the Christians in Ephesians 3:10, must not be overlooked. God's purpose is redemptive and God predetermined those in His church to participate in His purpose. We are to share the message of God's love, His wisdom, what gives life meaning, and who gives eternal life. This is the ultimate purpose God has laid upon His blood-bought church. It is this purpose that keeps life from being routine and meaningless.

God's purpose has far reaching consequences into eternity, and can be summed up in our making the treasures of God and His insight on eternal life known to others. When we tap into this aspect of God's purpose, we will find all the hope we will need in the "C" word moments of life. We will have the confidence to approach God in our time of need because we have aligned ourselves with God's purpose regardless of our current sufferings.

I told my friend that his faith in his trial had led him to see he needed to realign his purpose with God's purpose in spite of his trial. I explained how we could join with God in the greatest mission this world has ever known – making known *the manifold wisdom of God*. He agreed; he was a man of faith. We thanked God together that day and expressed our appreciation that God was, and is, a gracious God.

It was from this point on he found a hope that he had not fully found earlier in his Christian experience. Never again would he be guilty of mouthing the words of hope from the pages of the song book, without those words ringing out a melody in his heart first. He shared with others in his church family how easy it is to get sidetracked to God's Divine purpose for the church. The purpose of the church extends beyond praise and worship. It covers more than rubbing our shoulders and encouraging one another in fellowship.

The purpose that gets us out of life's rut in the first place is God's intent to save us. Once saved, we are to cooperate with God's eternal purpose which He made possible in Christ for us to spread the good news of Christ. We live in a world filled with hopelessness and people are trying to crowd God out – out of the schools, out of the homes, and out of everyday life. We who believe on the other hand must stand among the hopeless crowds, lifting high the cross of Christ, pronouncing the message of hope.

God has revealed His purpose and, in this purpose, we find hope and we extend hope to others. We are sharers together in the promise of Christ (Ephesians 3:6). Paul states in Ephesians 3, he became a servant of this good news and by grace he shared with others the unparalleled riches of Christ. *I became a servant of this gospel by the gift of God's grace given me through the working of his power... to preach to the Gentiles the unsearchable riches of Christ* (Ephesians 3:7-8). We can find hope by understanding God's passion for us and His purpose in us. We can be members together with God in one body and be united in His redemptive purpose in reaching the lost through the church.

Paul was given grace from God to proclaim God's grace to others. The forces of evil tried everything to get him sidetracked but his hope-filled life helped him stay on course to fill others with the hope-filled message of Christ. Colossians 1:25-27, *²⁵ I have become its servant by the commission God gave me to present to you the word of God in its fullness – ²⁶ the mystery that has been kept hidden for ages and generations, but is now disclosed to the saints. ²⁷ To them God has chosen to make known among the Gentiles the glorious riches of this mystery, which is Christ in you, the hope of glory.* There is a similar thread of information between these words in Colossians 1:25-27 and the words we read in Ephesians 3:7-13.

What God had done for Paul was so great that it had become the driving force in his life. Paul had become a part of God's mighty purpose and by grace we can join in God's mighty purpose. For example, Paul saw himself as a prisoner of Christ for the sake of the Gentile world (Ephesians 3:1). God's grace and rich mercy Paul spoke of in Ephesian chapters 1 and 2 captivated his life. God's grace snapped him out of his ho-hum religious routine as a Pharisee.

Paul learned that under the New Covenant the grace of God would be available to him only by believing that Jesus was the Christ. He finally repented of his rejection of Jesus when he realized only Christ could bring him into the righteousness of God. By grace Paul understood the promise of a hope-filled, purpose-filled life, only comes through faith in Christ.

Paul became a man with a mission and his mission was tied to God's purpose in the church – the purpose of making known how perfectly God's objective of His eternal purpose fits together in the church. Ephesians 3:10-11, *[10] His intent was that now, through the church, the manifold wisdom of God should be made known to the rulers and authorities in the heavenly realms, [11] according to his eternal purpose which he accomplished in Christ Jesus our Lord.*

It was God's intent that we, the church, be a people that spreads seeds of eternal hope. It was God's objective that the church be a place where the hopeless find hope. It was God's purpose that the church be the place where the confused find clarity of truth, the disillusioned find direction in life, and the broken-hearted find eternal encouragement. Together we can enjoy the unsearchable riches of Christ. Together we can be sharers together in God's redemptive purpose which brings endless hope.

My song leading friend was able to lead singing off and on for about eight months after his cancer diagnosis, which in itself was quite amazing. But it was not his song leading that the church appreciated most about this man. What we remember most about this man that blessed the congregation and everyone appreciated dearly was his inspiring testimony of Jesus. He connected to God's purpose of spreading the good news to his own life wherever he went. Every day and in every place, he reflected an incredible measure of substantial hope.

He wanted others to know this hope that comes from Christ. There is no greater purpose that will give our lives meaning and direction. The result of such hope is that our friend and fellow Christian song leader became the seed sower. In Luke

8 Jesus tells a parable about a Sower who sowed the Seed. When He was through describing how the seed was spread in the various landscapes, He explained those different soils were representative of different hearts. He told his disciples, *"The seed is the Word of God"* (Luke 8:11).

My heaven-bound friend took the seed God had given him and for the rest of his earthly days consciously tried to spread the seed of eternal hope. He began doing what God desires His people to do – make known *the manifold wisdom of God*. He embraced God's purpose with a renewed zeal and set a great example for other believers. In Acts 8, a great persecution broke out against the early church, which caused them to spread out through Judea and Samaria. Acts 8:4, *Those who had been scattered preached the word wherever they went*. The apostles remained in Jerusalem, but the church dispersed, naturally doing what God intended for her to do.

My friend and brother in Christ who battled cancer never complained about his disease. He faced one huge problem after another, but with such grace in his heart, and he did not want anybody else to lose their hope in the Lord over his trials. This was the attitude of another servant of God which happened to be the writer of Ephesians. *I ask you, therefore, not to be discouraged because of my sufferings for you, which are your glory* (Ephesians 3:13).

My seed sowing, song leading friend, inspires us to remember God's purpose which will lead us to experientially see the hope we can have in the unsearchable riches of Christ. The apostle Paul said it this way, *I am not ashamed of the gospel, because it is the power of God for the salvation of everyone who believes: first for the Jew, then for the Gentile* (Romans 1:16). When we have discovered the good news of Jesus in God's eternal purpose, we should naturally share it with others.

Some parents attend birthing classes prior to having their first child. My wife wanted me to go with her to some child prebirth classes that would teach us some healthy birth practices for childbirth and labor. The class was provided by the hospital in an effort to assist couples who were expecting a child. Basically, as I think back, the classes taught us to breath.

We were told if we would work together on relaxing and breathing, then my wife's potential labor pain would be greatly reduced. That interested her and pleased me so we continued to progress through the classes. We learned it would be possible for her to deliver our baby without the use of any pain killing drugs. Still something about taking classes on how to breathe seemed a bit preposterous to me, since I thought back then and still do that breathing is sort of natural.

During the several weeks of class we concentrated on various breathing techniques. We were told these techniques would be helpful during the delivery of our baby. If we would follow the breathing techniques it would make the birthing process more pleasant. Before we were done with our first class, we heard sounds like we have never heard before. The sounds were not exactly the sound of chanting, but they were strange breathing, chanting sounds.

We listened to the instructor. We read all the material and studied all sorts of different breathing techniques. We did deep breathing, pant breathing, slow breathing, and more. My wife wanted to give birth to our first child without any pain relieving drugs. Within the first hours of giving birth to our child she informed me that if there was going to be another child in our future, she was opting for the pain killers instead of the breathing classes. I completely understand her reasoning because when it came time for her to give birth, the fancy breathing techniques went right out the window.

I did notice one noteworthy thing during her intense pain of labor and that is she never forgot to breathe. Even during the most painful minutes of the birthing process she never forgot to breathe, she naturally breathed. The church of Christ that lines up with the heart of God and His eternal purpose will naturally do what God has designed her to do and that's share the good news. We do not have to be an eloquent speaker or good with words to share the good news of Jesus. But we will need to open our mouths and sow God's seed that will lead others to live a hope-filled life.

When God called Moses from the burning bush and told him to lead the Israelites out of slavery, Moses tried every excuse in the book to avoid being used. He did not feel qualified for such a task. He told God he did not know what to say and words were never his gift. We too have our excuses for not opening our mouths, but they are not sufficient in God's view. May we remember it is not our responsibility to make people believe. Our God given task is to sow the seed and make available the good news.

Spreading the seed does not have to be complicated. Sowing the seed should be natural thing, as natural to believers as our breathing. We do not have to stop and think every time we take a breath. When we are healthy, breathing is natural thing we do. When we are spiritually healthy and aligned to God's eternal purpose it will be natural for us to try to encourage others to follow Jesus and know the hope we enjoy.

If we desire to be co-laborers with the Lord, we will invest in people and invite them to follow Jesus. We will generously invest in people by showing them God's kind of love, care, and concern. We invest in people by sowing the seed of God's Word that promises perpetual dividends. There are times when someone walks into a church building without knowing anyone prior to their first visit; however, most people have been invited by someone before they visit a church assembly.

It is more likely that a person will visit a worship service, class, or some other church function like a fall celebration, after they have received a personal invitation. In fact, we may have needed multiple invitations, but thankfully the person did not give up on us. They kept investing in us, helping us, and continued throwing seeds of hope in our direction. We can invest in people and invite them to hear about God's eternal purpose without pressuring them.

The church exists for people. We invest in people by getting to know them and spending time with them. We share in their interests and share our interests with them. We invest in people by praying for them. I have noticed that if we offer to help our neighbors with some project around their house or some other skill we have, most people will let us help them. Unchurched people rarely walk into the church house and listen to a preacher without a personal invitation. When we invest in people's lives, they will more likely be receptive to the seeds of hope.

In the first century church in Ephesus, the Christians invested in people and invited others to join them in following the Lord. We must do whatever we can to share Christ with others and help others come to know the blessing of living a hope-filled life. There is a story in the Old Testament that has some valid application for us living under New Testament age. The story reminds us that once we have discovered good news – news that could help others – we would not be doing right if we did not try to share that good news with others.

The story is found in 2 Kings. The setting of the story was during the reign of King Ben-Hadad, the king of the Arameans. His army had surrounded God's people in the city of Samaria. He was permitting no food, water, or any life-sustaining provisions to enter the city. There was already a famine across the land and this evil king used the famine to his advantage. With relentless determination he planned to starve the people of God to the point of surrender.

The situation became so desperate in the city of Samaria that the Bible tells of two women who were so hungry actually resorting to cannibalism in an effort to survive. 2 Kings 6:26-29, *[26] As the king of Israel was passing by on the wall, a woman cried to him, "Help me, my lord the king!" [27] The king replied, "If the LORD does not help you, where can I get help for you? From the threshing floor? From the winepress?" [28] Then he asked her, "What's the matter?" She answered, "This woman said to me, 'Give up your son so we may eat him today, and tomorrow we'll eat my son.'* *²⁹ So we cooked my son and ate him. The next day I said to her, 'Give up your son so we may eat him,' but she had hidden him."*

It was a terrible, terrible situation! 2 Kings 7:3-4, *³ Now there were four men with leprosy at the entrance of the city gate. They said to each other, "Why stay here until we die? ⁴ If we say, 'We'll go into the city' – the famine is there, and we will die. And if we stay here, we will die. So let's go over to the camp of the Arameans and surrender. If they spare us, we live; if they kill us, then we die."*

Four lepers had thought through their options. They were either going to starve to death if they continued to sit there at the city gate, or possibly die upon surrendering to the Arameans. They had limited options, but there was at least a chance, slim as it might have been, that the Arameans might spare their lives. They decided they needed to do something and take what action was available to them. The lepers waited till twilight and made their move.

2 Kings 7:5-7, *⁵ At dusk they got up and went to the camp of the Arameans. When they reached the edge of the camp, not a man was there, ⁶ for the Lord had caused the Arameans to hear the sound of chariots and horses and a great army, so that they said to one another, "Look, the king of Israel has hired the Hittite and Egyptian kings to attack us!" ⁷ So they got up and fled in the dusk and abandoned their tents and their horses and donkeys. They left the camp as it was and ran for their lives.*

The lepers stepped out and God blessed their action. We realize that for them it was a step of desperation, but we should take note a couple of important things. 2 Kings 7:5, speaks of it being at "dusk" or "twilight" that lepers decided to get up and go into the Aramean camp. Then it indicates that in 2 Kings 7:7, it was "dusk" or "twilight" that the Aramean army fled in fear of their lives. In other words, at the exact time the lepers made their move, God went to work for them. Consequently, the lepers walked into the Syrian camp with their hands up ready to surrender, only to discover the camp had been abandoned.

Amazing results happened when the lepers decided to quit sitting around doing nothing and did something. No one was in the camp. Without any opposition they walked into the enemy's camp and found food and drink at their disposal. They filled their stomachs with the food, but it was not only food the Arameans had left behind. They left nearly everything behind which tells us they thought they needed to leave the camp as quickly as possible.

The lepers discovered all kinds of useful items. The found clothes and other treasures. They found gold and silver without having to mine for gold and silver. They began taking the items of value for themselves along with the precious metals and started hiding them. They moved from one tent to another collecting the valuables.

2 Kings 7:9-11, [9] *Then they said to each other, "We're not doing right. This is a day of good news and we are keeping it to ourselves. If we wait until daylight, punishment will overtake us. Let's go at once and report this to the royal palace."* [10] *So they went and called out to the city gatekeepers and told them, "We went into the Aramean camp and not a man was there*

—not a sound of anyone – only tethered horses and donkeys, and the tents left just as they were." [11] *The gatekeepers shouted the news, and it was reported within the palace.*

The lepers realized God had blessed them with good news and good news was meant to be shared. These men understood there was such a thing as the sin of silence. James 4:17, *Anyone, then, who knows the good he ought to do and doesn't do it, sins.* The ancient story from 2 Kings has a message for us Christians. We have found spiritual food and drink and discovered the unsearchable riches of Christ – those riches must be shared.

The Lord has graciously brought hope to our souls. We who have experienced the good news of Jesus would be doing wrong if we just keep that wonderful news to ourselves. We are tempted to sit around and do nothing when we should be doing whatever we can to spread the good news of hope that Jesus offers to all nations.

After Jesus' resurrection, He told his disciples some very specific words. Matthew 28:19-20, [19] *Therefore go and make disciples of all nations, baptizing them in the name of the Father and of the Son and of the Holy Spirit,* [20] *and teaching them to obey everything I have commanded you. And surely, I am with you always, to the very end of the age.* The word translated "nations" in verse 19, is from the Greek word ETHNOS. We get our English word "ethnic," from this Greek word.

ETHNOS includes we are to do what we can to make everyone followers of Jesus. All peoples, all places, and all languages need to hear the hope-filled news. The disciples that first heard the words in Matthew 28:19-20, likely felt overwhelmed at first with such a command, but God would be with them to spread His powerful seed. The charge to the church is to make disciples and we are reminded of the Lord's purpose, and our responsibility in the church. The words from the Lord in Matthew 28 are sometimes referred to as "The Great Commission."

May we find comfort in that we are not alone in this mission. We already knew that Jesus was with us, but the Lord made a special promise prior to His ascending back into heaven. When we go sowing the seed that will make disciples, He will be with us always! When we speak to people about Jesus' carrying out the two-fold principle of investing and inviting, Jesus goes with us as we put our part of the "go" in the gospel. This is the day of good news and we cannot keep the hope we have found in God's purpose to ourselves.

CHAPTER 8 – QUESTIONS
TO DISCUSS, DEVELOP, AND DETERMINE

1. What is God's purpose for the church according to Ephesians 3:10? Describe the result of carrying out that purpose.

2. What is God's purpose that initially gets us out of life's sin rut in the first place? What are we to do after receiving and accepting the good news in our lives?

3. Name four things unchurched people ought to be able to find in the church.

4. What lesson can we learn from the Christians (Acts 8) that had been scattered across the country due to the intense persecution?

5. Name two things we can do on a practical level to be co-laborers with the Lord in His mission.

6. Explain the seriousness of the situation God's people found themselves in when they were surrounded by the Aramean army.

7. What did the four lepers decide to do and why? What was the initial result of their actions and what did they finally do?

8. What English word do we get from the Greek word ETHNOS? Explain what Ethnos is trying to get across as we align ourselves with God's purpose.

FIND HOPE IN GOD'S PLEA FOR UNITY
(Ephesians 4:1-16)

What freedom do we Christians enjoy now as citizens of the United States that we would most hate to lose? Let us consider this question as we begin to survey the early verses in Ephesians 4. We are blessed to be citizens of this country. We enjoy many freedoms that just do not exist in other places. What privilege, what right, what freedom would bother us the most to lose?

As Americans we enjoy many blessings that are not an inherent right in other countries. There are countries that are run by dictators and governments where an individual cannot move around freely. People in some countries are told where to live and are told what they will do for work. We take these basic things for granted because of the freedoms we enjoy in this country.

Let us consider something else, as we consider how we might answer the question, "What privilege, right, or freedom would bother us the most to lose?" Consider how the Apostle Paul might answer such a question. He was commissioned by God to make God's plea for unity to the Christians meeting in Ephesus. Ephesians 4:1-3, *¹ As a prisoner for the Lord, then, I urge you to live a life worthy of the calling you have received. ² Be completely humble and gentle; be patient, bearing with one another in love. ³ Make every effort to keep the unity of the Spirit through the bond of peace.*

Paul identified himself *as a prisoner for the Lord*. If we can try to look through the lens Paul gives us as he begins chapter 4, we will gain some valuable insight into how he might answer the question. Paul was a Jew, a Roman citizen, and before he became a Christian, a persecutor of those who followed Jesus. Paul was a distinguished leader among the Jews, and had held considerable influence in the Jewish synagogues and with the Sanhedrin counsel in Jerusalem prior to becoming a Christian. The Sanhedrin counsel carried supreme Jewish authority. The Sanhedrin could have Jewish people arrested, tried, and sentenced in their court.

The Sanhedrin administered civil jurisdiction and ruled as the authority on Jewish law. The Jews who lived under Roman rule could function and practice their Jewish faith as long as they obeyed the laws of Rome. As much power as the Sanhedrin had among the Jews they still had to function under the power of Rome's law. For example, they were typically not allowed to put anyone to death without Rome's permission.

Paul was a Jew who had been born in Tarsus which gave him Roman citizenship. He had many rights and privileges as a citizen. For example, a Roman citizen had the right to be tried in court against any charge. If he was then found guilty, he would be sentenced to punishment by the Roman authorities. Anyone without citizenship could be immediately punished if accused of a crime. For example, after becoming a Christian Paul found himself transitioning from being the persecutor to being among those being persecuted for their faith in Christ.

In Acts 21, a crowd of Jews got stirred up because they believed Paul had betrayed the Jewish faith by promoting the name of Jesus. Paul was accused of being the instigator for the public disturbance and the news reached the ears of Roman commander. Paul was arrested due to all the commotion. Rome let the Jews function as long as they were peaceful and stayed within the bounds of Roman law. As the soldiers were leading Paul away, he requested to speak once more to the crowd. Paul was given permission (Acts 21:40), but the commander was still unaware he was a Roman citizen.

Paul shared his background and in brevity his conversion story of how he became a follower of Jesus. The crowd of Jews again did not like what they heard and it reenergized the disturbance. The commander quickly got a grip on the out of control situation and ordered Paul to be taken away to be flogged. When Paul notified the centurion in charge of the flogging that he was a Roman citizen, there was an immediate pause to the flogging. The centurion became concerned when he discovered Paul was a Roman citizen.

Acts 22:25-29, [25] *As they stretched him out to flog him, Paul said to the centurion standing there, "Is it legal for you to flog a Roman citizen who hasn't even been found guilty?"* [26] *When the centurion heard this, he went to the commander and reported it. "What are you going to do?" he asked. "This man is a Roman citizen."* [27] *The commander went to Paul and asked, "Tell me, are you a Roman citizen?" "Yes, I am," he answered.* [28] *Then the commander said, "I had to pay a big price for my citizenship." "But I was born a citizen," Paul replied.* [29] *Those who were about to question him withdrew immediately. The commander himself was alarmed when he realized that he had put Paul, a Roman citizen, in chains.*

Paul saw himself not as a prisoner of Rome, but as a prisoner of the Lord. Paul voluntarily chose to be in the Lord's army. Regardless of who might arrest him he would boldly claim his loyalty. He was not simply a prisoner of Rome, or of the Sanhedrin, but rather of the Lord Jesus Christ. The Lord had not arrested Paul like the Roman commander. The Lord had not twisted his arm to make him declare those words. I believe his identifying statement in Ephesians 4:1 – a prisoner for the Lord, gives some valuable insight into how he might answer the question as to what right he would most hate to lose.

With Paul's identifying committed mindset to the Lord we might be able to conclude Paul would not want to lose his right to speak up for Jesus. Paul had the right as a Roman citizen to speak and preach about Jesus. This was the right I believe he would most want to keep. However, if Paul had lost the Roman privilege as a citizen to speak up for Jesus and share with others the good news of Christ, there is no doubt he would have continued to tell others about Jesus. Why? Because he was willing to be a prisoner for the Lord.

No matter how much the Sanhedrin persecuted him, and irrespective of how much the stubborn Jewish leadership tried to oppress him to stop speaking the name of Jesus, Paul persisted. The Sanhedrin had ordered other apostles not to speak anymore in the name of Jesus, but Paul held the same view of Peter and John. Acts 4:18-20, [18] *Then they [Sanhedrin] called them in again and commanded them not to speak or teach at all in the name of Jesus.* [19] *But Peter and John replied, "Judge for yourselves whether it is right in God's sight to obey you rather than God.* [20] *For we cannot help speaking about what we have seen and heard."*

The Christians in Acts 4 and 5 were in danger of losing the most precious right they had in their day, the right to worship the Lord and tell others about Jesus. The Sanhedrin court made it known that no one was to proclaim Jesus. Nonetheless, Peter, John, Paul, and other believers continued to speak of Jesus, regardless of any restrictions placed upon them. The early Christians spoke the name of Christ, in spite of suffering physical persecution at times.

Today we have the privilege to freely voice the name of Jesus and worship the Lord. Let us not take these blessings and privileges for granted. Not everyone appreciates our having the right to proclaim Jesus is Lord. There are individuals, and groups, who want to oppress and suppress our Christian privileges. Thankfully, we still live in a country where we do not have to fear physical death for mentioning Jesus. Thankfully, we can pray and worship in the name of Jesus even though some oppose our belief.

There are unbelievers who make fun of us, and in some cases do worse things to us. Back to our question, what right do we now enjoy as a citizen of this land that we would most hate to lose? Would it not be the right to speak freely of Jesus and to worship Jesus freely? We are blessed to be able to speak the name of Jesus without being arrested or killed for our belief. Yes, we face difficulties at time and persecution comes our way at times even from those who call themselves believers.

What a blessing we enjoy to live in a nation where we can freely speak our faith in Jesus, which cannot be done freely in other places in the world. There is so much disunity in our world, and even in the religious world, that various types of persecution will be inevitable at times. But when we speak up for the Lord, we are living an honorable life worthy of our Christian calling. *As a prisoner for the Lord, then, I urge you to live a life worthy of the calling you have received* (Ephesians 4:1).

Let us join the early disciples who loved the Lord and out of their love for others share God's plea for unity. There is hope in understanding God's plea for us to be a united people. We can be united in Jesus, but this unity requires us to have the desire to worship the Lord in spirit and truth. The idea of having the right is apparent in the wording of Ephesians 4:2-3, *² Be completely humble and gentle; be patient, bearing with one another in love. ³ Make every effort to keep the unity of the Spirit through the bond of peace.*

We have been brought together by Christ and made members of one another. Together we are to work toward being unified citizens of heaven. We can do this as a result of the bond the Lord made possible by way of His blood. How can we be united? By being humble and submissive to the Lord's model for unity. Humility comes from encountering God. The more humble, gentle, and patient we are, the easier it will be for us to be united in the Lord.

As God's people we honor God and bless ourselves when we look to God's Word for answers to bring us together rather than to divide us. We are to bear with one another in love and that necessitates a willingness to be humble, gentle, and patient with each other as the Lord is patient with us.

We must get rid of any selfish motivations and make individual and collective effort so we can remain united through the bond of peace.

Selfishness and pride, like other sins, can still crop up on the other side of the waters of baptism. Our responsibility before God is when these sins show up in our lives, we rush to repent of them. By continuing to lean on God's mercy in our effort to be humble, gentle, and patient we will stay on salvation's road. What a blessing it is to be a people who believe in God and will exert personal effort to glorify God by our actions as a result of that belief.

The Greek verb translated *"make every effort"* in Ephesians 1:3, carries the idea of effort combined with eagerness. Paul is saying that every disciple must show diligence in our commitment to keep unity. If unity were easily maintained and sustained, there would be no need for this direction by the Holy Spirit. Unity will only have a chance if we expend our energies to be unified. But keeping unity at the cost of comprising Bible truth is not what is meant here.

We must not buy into the prevailing lie among many today. We have all heard the lie that, "There are no moral absolutes in this world." That is a lie and the furthest thing from what is taught in Scripture. God has absolutes and one of the most obvious absolutes is that the wages of sin is death. Everyone has fallen short of God's absolutes. To ignore that God has established moral and Biblical absolutes, and that we need to repent of sin, is to have bought into Satan's lies.

Unity God's way can only happen if we will stay with His fundamental essentials for our having unity. To have unity, of course, we need the right spirit, but we also need to acknowledge God's truth. Truth matters. When I was much younger, I never understood why people would use a pill dispenser. The little plastic pill boxes with individual compartments labeled by the different days of the week seemed like just another way to get our money. Now I am of the age I understand completely how beneficial a pill organizer can be.

When was the last time we wondered if we had taken our designated pills for the day? I recently found myself wondering, did I take the pill or not. My view has changed toward the daily pill boxes. These little boxes are practical and helpful. In fact, they can even save lives. There are certain pills we cannot double up on without causing serious health issues. If we think we took our pill for the day, and we did not take it, that can also result in a serious health complication. If the truth matters when it comes to our taking a single pill, then how much more does it matter when it comes to our eternal souls.

When we hear the word "unity" in Ephesians 1:3, several other words may come to our minds. We may think of words like consensus, harmony, agreement, peace, and solidarity. When I hear the word unity, I think of the word oneness. The idea of oneness fits the context. Jew and Gentile have been brought together into one body. Ephesians 4:4-6, *4 There is one body and one Spirit – just as you were called to one hope when you were called – 5 one Lord, one faith, one baptism; 6 one God and Father of all, who is over all and through all and in all.*

The oneness that brings God's kind of unity and hope to us does not come from only having the right spirit and attitude, or even by extending our effort. Oneness is dependent upon our willingness to acknowledge and obey the foundational principles of unity in Ephesians 4:4-6. God is pleased when members of His body are making the effort to be united in His oneness and truth. God expects the members of His one Body to desire to worship Him in spirit and truth.

There is one body and the one body is the church. There is nothing more beautiful than a unified church family. God has designed us in the one body to share together in living a hope-filled life. When we follow God's imperatives, we will enjoy spiritual healthy lives. God's blueprint for the church is that we will work together, spread seeds of hope, and help each other to mature our faith in the one body.

Ephesians 4:7-16, *⁷ But to each one of us grace has been given as Christ apportioned it. ⁸ This is why it says: "When he ascended on high, he led captives in his train and gave gifts to men." ⁹ (What does "he ascended" mean except that he also descended to the lower, earthly regions? ¹⁰ He who descended is the very one who ascended higher than all the heavens, in order to fill the whole universe.) ¹¹ It was he who gave some to be apostles, some to be prophets, some to be evangelists, and some to be pastors and teachers, ¹² to prepare God's people for works of service, so that the body of Christ may be built up ¹³ until we all reach unity in the faith and in the knowledge of the Son of God and become mature, attaining to the whole measure of the fullness of Christ. ¹⁴ Then we will no longer be infants, tossed back and forth by the waves, and blown here and there by every wind of teaching and by the cunning and craftiness of men in their deceitful scheming. [15] Instead, speaking the truth in love, we will in all things grow up into him who is the Head, that is, Christ. [16] From him the whole body, joined and held together by every supporting ligament, grows and builds itself up in love, as each part does its work.*

There is no limit to what God will do through His body if we will hold fast to God's plan for oneness. We can join Jesus in church growth in His body by keeping His plea for unity in our local congregation. As we work together, we are doing bodybuilding God's way. Spiritual exercise coupled with the right attitude will help us to mature together. The message of Christ's growth plan through the church fills us with hope as we join together, grow together, and work together.

All members in the church are to do their part to mature in the faith and work in harmony with the rest of the body. At times we may be tempted to think things that take us away from our individual responsibility of doing our part in the Lord's work, which is unhelpful and sinful. We may think things like, if the church would do this or that we would be stronger and healthier. We may think that if the leadership would do this or that the church would be more fruitful and united. We may think if the deacons would do this or that we would be one. We may think if we had this program or these activities, we could be united, when our unity is actually the result of following the directives of oneness and bodybuilding in Ephesians 4.

The church is not filled with perfect preachers, elders, deacons, or members. The church is filled with people who have acknowledged their need for the Lord's mercy and have found hope in the unified family of God. The unity and the health of the local church depends on our doing our part. Our responsibility to do our part is often shifted from ourselves to somebody else that we think is not doing their part. Every member of the body will be held accountable to God. Let us do our part and be a supporting member striving to build up the whole body.

God made sure the church would have what she would need to mature and become spiritually strong in the faith. God gave the early church the inspired apostles, some prophets, some evangelists, and some pastor-teachers with a purpose in mind – to prepare God's people for works of service. Therefore, they would no longer be infants in the faith blown around by the latest doctrinal teaching that blew their direction. God's design in gifting the church was to help her stay united and connected to the Head of the church, which is Christ.

The apostles and prophets fulfilled special roles in the foundation of the church. In view of the needs of the early church the apostles who revealed God's truth were in reality gifts to the church. Even today the apostles' teaching we have in the Bible guides us. We also learn that God gave the church evangelists and pastor-teachers. The Greek word POIMEN in Ephesians 4:11, is translated "pastors" in several Bible translations (King James Version, The New King James, The New American Standard Bible, and the New International Version). In every other place in these translations translate the word POIMEN with the word "shepherd."

The Greek word POIMEN carries the idea of tending to a flock of sheep or feeding sheep. It is noteworthy the English Stand Version translates the word POIMEN, "shepherds," in Ephesians 4:11. The Greek word was one of the specific words used for the work of elders in the church. It carries the idea of feeding and tending to a flock of sheep – God's sheep. The apostle Paul called the elders at Ephesus to meet him in Miletus (Acts 20:17) and there he admonished them to be alert and continue to work at maturing the Christian flock.

Paul said, *28 Keep watch over yourselves and all the flock of which the Holy Spirit has made you overseers. Be shepherds of the church of God, which he bought with his own blood. 29 I know that after I leave, savage wolves will come in among you and will not spare the flock. 30 Even from your own number men will arise and distort the truth in order to draw away disciples after them* (Acts 20:28-30). Distorting and twisting the truth is not something new in our day. Paul knew these elders well and he knew they believed the truth, practiced the truth, but they also needed to guard the truth.

The pastors or elders in Ephesians 4, were teachers who served the Lord in the church alongside evangelists or preachers for a defined purpose. The purpose of God giving gifts to the church is to mature and prepare people for works of service. Maturity develops over time, but Christian ministry should begin on the first day we become a Christian. Ephesians 4:12-13, *12 to prepare God's people for works of service, so that the body of Christ may be built up 13 until we all reach unity in the faith and in the knowledge of the Son of God and become mature, attaining to the whole measure of the fullness of Christ.*

The one body is linked to six other absolute identifying marks centered around the theme of oneness. Note that in addition to there being one body there is one Spirit. The one Spirit is the Holy Spirit of God. A person cannot be in a saved relationship today without possessing the indwelling Spirit. Romans 8:9, *You, however, are not in the flesh but in the Spirit, if in fact the Spirit of God dwells in you. Anyone who does not have the Spirit of Christ does not belong to him* (English Standard Version). We have already noted in Ephesians 1:13, Christians are marked with a seal and the seal is the Holy Spirit of promise. We receive the indwelling gift of the Holy Spirit when we obey the same gospel that was preached on the day of Pentecost in Acts 2.

There is one hope. This is the hope that makes all the difference in the world. This hope is a living hope that Peter speaks of in 1 Peter 1:3. We have been blessed with a life-giving hope that is unwaveringly rooted and grounded in a living relationship with God the Father, God the Son, and God the Holy Spirit. The living hope helps us to live beyond life's obstacles. The church has a message of hope that extends beyond our strength as we rely on God's strength working through us.

There is one Lord. When there is one Lord, we can know with absolute certainty there are not two. One day, every knee will bow to the one Lord. One day, every tongue will confess that Jesus Christ is the one Lord. If we wait till that momentous day before we acknowledge the Lord by our words and actions, it will be too late to change our eternal destiny. But for those who stand one with the Lord and in the power of Lord's oneness in His unified Body will know eternal hope.

There is one faith. When the New Testament speaks of one faith it refers to the thing believed rather than the act of believing. The one faith is not referring to our personal faith, but the body of teaching that has been delivered through the apostles (John 16:13). The one faith is the faith that can be preached according to Galatians 1:23. It is the one faith that can be obeyed according to Acts 6:7. The one faith is the faith that we can remain true to according to Acts 14:22. The power of oneness is demonstrated when the church takes the one faith and grows up in Christ (Ephesians 4:15-16).

There is one baptism. Christian baptism is a burial in water prompted by faith in God's command. This is the baptism Jesus commanded His apostles to teach following His resurrection. Mark 16:16, *Whoever believes and is baptized will be saved, but whoever does not believe will be condemned.* The one baptism is the one Peter and apostles preached on the day the church began. When the crowd asked Peter and the other apostles what to do in light of learning that they had responsibility in crucifying Jesus who was declared to be the resurrected Lord he said, *"Repent and be baptized, every one of you, in the name of Jesus Christ for the forgiveness of your sins. And you will receive the gift of the Holy Spirit"* (Acts 2:38).

The one baptism was preached by the apostles and practiced by the early church. The one baptism is an immersion in water. The conversion example in Acts 8 illustrates baptism was by immersion. An Ethiopian had traveled to Jerusalem in a chariot to worship and on his way home he was reading the prophet Isaiah. Acts 8:35, *Then*

Philip began with that very passage of Scripture and told him the good news about Jesus. By God's providence Phillip was able to sit down with him and tell him the good news of Jesus that brings hope.

Undoubtedly Phillip's hope-filled message of Jesus had something to do with baptism. I say that based on what we can read in the Bible. Acts 8:36, 38-39, *[36] As they traveled along the road, they came to some water and the eunuch said, "Look, here is water. Why shouldn't I be baptized?" [38] And he gave orders to stop the chariot. Then both Philip and the eunuch went down into the water and Philip baptized him. [39] When they came up out of the water, the Spirit of the Lord suddenly took Philip away, and the eunuch did not see him again, but went on his way rejoicing.* Notice they went down into the water in verse 38 and came up out of the water in verse 39.

There is one body, one Spirit, one hope, one Lord, one faith, and one baptism. There is one more identifying statement added to the list of one's. Ephesians 4:6 adds there is, *one God and Father of all, who is over all and through all and in all.* This one God calls us to the one faith, that unites us together in one body, when we are baptized into the one Lord, as a result of God's revelation from the one Spirit which fills us with one special kind of hope. 1 Corinthians 12:13, *For we were all baptized by one Spirit into one body – whether Jews or Greeks, slave or free – and we were all given the one Spirit to drink.*

As we close out this chapter let me remind us of something very important. Everyone needs hope, but they need a living hope. The gulf between the hopeless and the hopeful is linked by the saving grace of God represented by our being unified in the seven one's found in Ephesians 4:4-6. Within those seven we find the word hope. The one hope is surrounded by a company of ones that unite God's people in His truth.

Christian compassion meets people where they are, but truth matters. The Bible says in John 8:31-32, *31 To the Jews who had believed him, Jesus said, "If you hold to my teaching, you are really my disciples. 32 Then you will know the truth, and the truth will set you free."* The One God, one Lord, and One Spirit, is filled with compassion for lost souls who have no hope. The church needs to embrace the compassion of the Father, Son, and Holy Spirit as we offer hope for today, tomorrow, and for eternity. But may we also remember that compassion without truth sets no one free.

CHAPTER 9 – QUESTIONS
TO DISCUSS, DEVELOP, AND DETERMINE

1. Explain why Paul saw himself as a prisoner of the Lord. Regardless of who might have physically arrested Paul, what would he boldly claim? What do you think he would have done if had had lost his right to freely speak of Jesus as a Roman citizen?

2. What privilege or right do Christians living in the United States have that Christians in other parts of the world may not enjoy? In addition to thanking God for this right, what can we do to live honorable lives worthy of our calling?

3. We can be united in Jesus, but what does this unity require of us?

4. What are some essential attitudes we need to be united? When it comes to being united, what else matters and why does it matter?

5. What is our oneness as believers in the Lord dependent upon?

6. How can we do bodybuilding God's way? The message of Christ's growth plan through the church fills us with hope as we do three things. What are these three things?

7. What was God's purpose for giving gifts to the church?

8. Name six other absolute identifying marks centered around the theme of oneness that is linked to the one body.

FIND HOPE IN GOD'S PLEA FOR PURITY
(Ephesians 4:17-5:7)

We all would agree that experience is a good teacher, even if we had a bad experience. When I was seventeen years old, my main mode of transportation was a motorcycle. One weekend I took a trip on the motorcycle up into the mountains of the northern part of Arizona. It was a beautiful, relaxing ride. I pulled off the highway to get some gas in one of the smaller towns, and as I was traveling along the access road, I had to cross some gravel that was between the highway and the gas station.

As soon as I hit the gravel area, I heard what must have been a large rock slam underneath my frame or tailpipe. I was surprised I heard the sound of the rock above my loud exhaust pipes. As soon as I heard the sound I wondered if the rock had dented my new, shiny chrome tailpipe exhausts. As I was slowing down and pulling into the gas station, I reached down with one hand to feel along the surface of the tailpipe to see if could detect a dent. In no time, I had burned the skin right off the tips of my first three fingers, and I was wearing a glove! This was not one of my better decisions.

I learned from that painful experience how to correctly check an exhaust tailpipe for dents. We all have thought and done some pretty foolish things. There is a phrase found in Ephesians 4:17, that reminds us of a more serious kind of foolishness. The New International Version reads, *"futility of their thinking."* The English Standard Version reads, *"futility of their mind."*

The word "futility" means "useless." When something is futile it is meaningless and holds no profitable value. The word futility in the Ephesian context has to do with the process of a way a person thinks, which affects their actions. If a person's thinking is futile then their actions will likely be futile as well.

Ephesians 4:17-21, [17] *So I tell you this, and insist on it in the Lord, that you must no longer live as the Gentiles do, in the futility of their thinking.* [18] *They are darkened in their understanding and separated from the life of God because of the ignorance that is in them due to the hardening of their hearts.* [19] *Having lost all sensitivity, they have given themselves over to sensuality so as to indulge in every kind of impurity, with a continual lust for more.* [20] *You, however, did not come to know Christ that way.* [21] *Surely you heard of him and were taught in him in accordance with the truth that is in Jesus.*

If we are going to find hope in this life, we will need to change the futile thinking and actions of our past. How can we as Christians change the thinking that holds no spiritual or practical value? We can do this by putting on the wardrobe God has designed for His pure and holy people. We will explore God's dress code before we are finished with this chapter. At this point let us zero in on the idea of purity. Ephesians 5:3, *But among you there must not be even a hint of sexual immorality, or of any kind of impurity, or of greed, because these are improper for God's holy people.*

The idea of being holy is to be separated unto God. God's grace enables us to begin our Christian walk and as we walk in hope, we must line up our thinking and actions according to God's will. There is no hope for those who after becoming Christians continue to walk in the futility of worldly thinking. We need to develop a new and pure way of thinking which comes about by appreciating God's purifying us from our sins.

The King James Version in Ephesians 4:19, inserts the word "uncleanness" in the text while other translations use the word "impurity." These words are used as opposites to the words "clean" and "pure." The Greek word translated "pure" or "clean" is KATHAROS. This Greek word meant "without impurities." It was commonly used to purify the mind and emotions by cleansing it from contamination. This is the idea behind the Beatitude in Matthew 5:8 when Jesus said, "*Blessed are the pure in heart, for they will see God.*"

When our hearts have been cleansed and changed through faith in Christ, the pure in heart will be focused on God. Purity in heart brings hope into our life. This hope comes from being able to walk with God and being able to see God. Jesus' statement in Matthew 5:8 is not confined to seeing God one day in glory. Seeing God brings hope. Seeing God is a blessing the pure in heart can begin to experience now.

Jesus is also telling us the pure in heart will begin seeing God in this life. When our lives are focused on pleasing God and embracing the right attitudes in our walk in Him, we will see God. We will see his handiwork in the changing of seasons. We see God as we go about our daily activities of life. We see God in the birth of a child. We will see God in the church. We will see God in our prayers as we listen to Him through His Word. We will see God in the good times and in our times of trouble.

We would never be able to see God in this inspiring way and get our hearts clean without God's doing His spiritual heart cleansing on us in the first place. We would never get our sinful mess clean without Jesus. The cross of Christ was all about God cleaning us up and how God could keep us clean day by day (1 John 1:7). The cross made possible that people could be made pure and then live holy lives.

Hebrews 10:10-14, *[10] ...we have been made holy through the sacrifice of the body of Jesus Christ once for all. [11] Day after day every priest stands and performs his religious duties; again, and again he offers the same sacrifices, which can never take away sins. [12] But when this priest had offered for all time one sacrifice for sins, he sat down at the right hand of God. [13] Since that time he waits for his enemies to be made his footstool, [14] because by one sacrifice he has made perfect forever those who are being made holy.* God makes us functionally holy by His work on the cross.

God grants us a functional holiness and positional purity through the blood of Christ. The positional purity is the good news that puts sinners in the place where they can experience a life free from sin's penalty and be pure in heart. Spiritual cleansing brings us hope. We have been made pure and holy and we are being made pure and holy. Positional purity and functional holiness are designed to be practical and useful in our walk with God.

We can live pure and holy lives, not sinless lives or perfect lives, but we can live separated unto God and focused on doing His will. Purity and holiness are not about our skills, or abilities; they are about our relationship with God. Purity and holiness are incredible benefits that are ours as the result of Jesus' sacrificial death. God has solved our sin problem and our self-esteem problem by identifying us as His holy children.

As a result of God's actions of His grace upon us we have changed, and are forever changing the way we think about things and do things. We now can live hope-filled lives as we cooperate with God (Ephesians 4:23-24). There is hope to be found in the renewing of our attitudes and minds. The transformation of a renewed mind brings hope, meaning, and value to our life in Christ.

Philippians 2:5, *Your attitude should be the same as that of Christ Jesus*. We can mature in the mind of Christ as we allow our thoughts and actions to be directed by God's Word. 1 Peter 1:14, *As obedient children, do not conform to the evil desires you had when you lived in ignorance*. This is the point John made in 1 John 3:3, *Everyone who has this hope in him purifies himself, just as he is pure*.

When we who choose to marry get engaged, we quit dating other people because we are anticipating being with our future husband or wife. During the engagement period out of our love for our future spouse we behave properly. We do not want to leave a hint in the air that we are not in committed love with the one we are engaged to marry. The hope we have of joining together with our fiancée affects what we say and how we live our daily lives.

There is a practical purifying process attached to hope. Hope of being with the one we love controls our decisions and encourages us to live morally upright lives. When we are engaged to someone or even after we are married to someone, it is not possible to always be together. But hope, coupled in love, has an impact on the way we live when we are able to be together in person. Hope helps us keep our minds clean and our thoughts pure. Hope can help us maintain healthy relationships with everyone.

Ephesians 5:1-7, [1] *Be imitators of God, therefore, as dearly loved children* [2] *and live a life of love, just as Christ loved us and gave himself up for us as a fragrant offering and sacrifice to God.* [3] *But among you there must not be even a hint of sexual immorality, or of any kind of impurity, or of greed, because these are improper for God's holy people.* [4] *Nor should there be obscenity, foolish talk or coarse joking, which are out of place, but rather thanksgiving.* [5] *For of this you can be sure: No immoral, impure or greedy person – such a man is an idolater – has any inheritance in the kingdom of Christ and of God.* [6] *Let no one deceive you with empty words, for because of such things God's wrath comes on those who are disobedient.* [7] *Therefore do not be partners with them.*

With whom are we going to be partners? Will we continue to partner with God and live a life of love holding on to our hope, or will we enroll in the school of worldliness? The school of this world teaches worldliness, not godliness. The school of this world teaches impurity, not purity. The world's system teaches it is better to get than to give. The world teaches us to look out only for ourselves and in the process, we harden our heart and lose all sensitivity to spiritual things.

The Lord's school is the school we enter from the moment we become Christians. In the Lord's school we begin the lifelong process of renewing our minds by walking or living in God's kind of love. We practice God's love and we try to imitate, follow, and mimic the godly example the Lord as left for us to follow. If we drop out of the school of Christian growth, we will by default reenter the futility of the world's system. Selfishness, thoughtlessness, impurity and the desire to get more and more without concern for the needs of others is the world's system.

God called us out of the world, placed us in His church, gave us hope, and provided us the clothes of Christ's righteousness. Therefore, let us take to heart Romans 13:13-14, *13 Let us behave decently, as in the daytime, not in orgies and drunkenness, not in sexual immorality and debauchery, not in dissension and jealousy. 14 Rather, clothe yourselves with the Lord Jesus Christ, and do not think about how to gratify the desires of the sinful nature.* When we clothe ourselves in the Lord it substantially shapes the worthwhile ways we think about people, talk to people, and treat people.

1 John 3:7, *Dear children, do not let anyone lead you astray. He who does what is right is righteous, just as he is righteous.* John is reminding us sin is a big deal and we need to take sin seriously if we want to preserve our hope in Christ. The hope we have of one day being able to see God and to be with God causes us to try to do what is right and please Christ now.

Hope gives us something to look forward to and helps purify how we live in the present. With this in mind let us return to the wardrobe of attitudes and actions God has designed for us to put on in the place of our former sinful dress. The Lord's school is the school of putting off the old worldly ways and putting on the new ways outlined by God.

The purifying process is described by putting off the old sinful wardrobe and putting on the new garments of true righteousness and holiness. Ephesians 4:22-25, *22 You were taught, with regard to your former way of life, to put off your old self, which is being corrupted by its deceitful desires; 23 to be made new in the attitude of your minds; 24 and to put on the new self, created to be like God in true righteousness and holiness. 25 Therefore each of you must put off falsehood and speak truthfully to his neighbor, for we are all members of one body.*

The putting off and putting on curriculum demands we change our thoughts, words, and actions. Of course, this is not brand-new teaching in Ephesians. God's curriculum for His people has always had a three-point emphasis: thoughts, words, and actions. We cannot continue to follow the value system of the world. The world's value system is of no profitable value when it comes to our spiritual life with God. We cannot pattern ourselves after the unsaved, because the unsaved are without hope and separated from the saving grace of God.

Practice makes perfect in many areas of life. Christians who desire to walk with Christ need to practice, practice, practice, in doing right things. We need to practice in thinking right, talking right, and acting right. We need to take what God teaches us and put that teaching into practice. The way we think is important. We need to put off those thoughts that will spiritually hinder us and put on the thoughts that will spiritually strengthen us.

It is vital that we give careful consideration to the words we use with people. When we lie, we are following the curriculum of Satan. When we speak the truth, we are following the Lord's curriculum. Lying may be the norm in this world, but it is unacceptable to the pure in heart. Lying is lying and God hates liars. Proverbs 6:16-19, *[16] There are six things the LORD hates, seven that are detestable to him: [17] haughty eyes, a lying tongue, hands that shed innocent blood, [18] a heart that devises wicked schemes, feet that are quick to rush into evil, [19] a false witness who pours out lies and a man who stirs up dissension among brothers.*

There are some additional things the Proverb writer reminds us to put on our put-off list in addition to lying. However, since most of us came from a world where lying was regularly tolerated and, in many cases accepted, we must understand God's view on the subject. Lying is unacceptable to God. Revelation 21:8 reads, *[8] But the cowardly, the unbelieving, the vile, the murderers, the sexually immoral, those who practice magic arts, the idolaters and all liars – their place will be in the fiery lake of burning sulfur. This is the second death."*

It may be common today for people to lie to each other, to become bitterly angry with each other, and to take advantage of each other; but Christians must practice taking off such evil behavior. When we take these things off, we must replace them with the proper dress of righteousness. We should not forget that some who were now in the church at Ephesus had previously been liars, thieves, greedy, and impure; but now they were choosing to follow God's curriculum.

Ephesians 4:26-32, [26] *"In your anger do not sin": Do not let the sun go down while you are still angry,* [27] *and do not give the devil a foothold.* [28] *He who has been stealing must steal no longer, but must work, doing something useful with his own hands, that he may have something to share with those in need.* [29] *Do not let any unwholesome talk come out of your mouths, but only what is helpful for building others up according to their needs, that it may benefit those who listen.* [30] *And do not grieve the Holy Spirit of God, with whom you were sealed for the day of redemption.* [31] *Get rid of all bitterness, rage and anger, brawling and slander, along with every form of malice.* [32] *Be kind and compassionate to one another, forgiving each other, just as in Christ God forgave you.*

The Christians in Ephesus found hope in Christ and their hope led them to practice a life of purity before God. They practiced a lifestyle of purity by rejecting worldliness and pursuing holiness. They rejected sinful anger and refused to give the devil a foothold. They practiced pure living by sharing with those in need and tossing hurtful speech that easily leads to the intent of doing evil. They practiced a pure lifestyle by kicking bitterness out the door and replacing it with forgiveness.

We are told to forgive others as God forgave us in Christ. How did Christ forgive us? Completely. He did not hold anything back and that news fills our hearts with hope. Jesus displayed a passionate willingness to sacrifice His life so we could be forgiven. The principle of forgiving just as Christ forgave us is the principle we are to follow.

If we are going to follow Christ and imitate His love, we are going to have to practice His kind of forgiveness, kindness, and compassion with one another. These are some of the wonderful attributes that make up the wardrobe of the pure in heart. The pure in heart have hope, and their hope is in seeing God.

CHAPTER 10 – QUESTIONS
TO DISCUSS, DEVELOP, AND DETERMINE

1. Explain how the word "futility" is used in the Ephesian context and how it affects our actions.

2. How can we as Christians change the thinking that holds no spiritual or practical value?

3. What is the meaning of the Greek word KATHAROS translated "pure" or "clean" and how was it commonly used in the New Testament? What blessing did Jesus extend to the pure in heart?

4. What is the result of God's actions of His grace upon us? What did John say everyone will do who has hope? Explain the practical purifying process attached to hope when it comes to having healthy relationships.

5. What does God's curriculum of putting off and on demand from us? What are some things we are to put off, and some things put on, as we dress ourselves in garments of righteousness?

6. What is the three-point emphasis of God's curriculum?

7. Name three things that Christians need to practice daily as they walk with Christ.

8. How did Christ forgive us? What did hope cause the Christians in Ephesus to do?

FIND HOPE IN GOD'S PRUDENCE

(Ephesians 5:8-20)

Years ago, I saw something someone did that I would venture to say no one else has ever seen before. I am sure if anyone ever did what I saw being done that day they would not readily admit it. The experience I witnessed firsthand was carried out by a faithful church secretary. Here is the context of what led up to what I saw that unforgettable day.

The secretary had gotten in her car to go to the post office, bank, or lunch; I really do not remember her destination. We had a brother in the church that regularly volunteered to work around the church building during the week. He mostly did projects inside the building, but from time to time he worked outside in the flower beds. He would pull weeds and water the flowers. He would also kill the unwanted grass growing up through the parking lot, along with many other projects.

This particular day he had been outside the building working and he left for lunch leaving some of his tools and equipment behind. He had been using an electric yard blower machine to blow the unwanted pulled weeds out of the flower garden. He was planning to come back and blow off the accumulation of trash that had collected under the portico where the staff parked their cars during the week.

The secretary had gone out just ahead of me to get in her car and I was heading toward the church doors to go to lunch. She had gotten into her car and showed no attention to the extension cord scattered out on the ground in front and around her car. One end of the extension cord was still plugged into the wall inside the church foyer and the other end was plugged in to an electric yard blower.

As I walked through the foyer and approached the exterior glass doors to go to lunch, I heard a very loud unusual sound outside the building. I hurriedly ran to the doors and I saw the remnants of an extension cord that had been ripped out of the foyer wall and was stuck on the inside of the exterior doors. The glass doors rattled and shook, but as I reached the doors they came to a stop.

I immediately looked out in the parking lot and I saw our faithful church secretary making this wide turn out in our parking a lot to head back towards the street. She was totally oblivious to the fact that she was dragging part of an extension cord that had wrapped around her tire. That was bad enough but the cord was still attached to the yard blower and that was noise I had heard earlier. The blower was bouncing up and down behind her car.

Immediately it was decision time for me. Do I let her drag the blower to the bank or the post office, or do I run out in the parking lot and wave my hands like a fool and try to get her attention? I decided I would try to flag her down. I chose to help her by running out there waving my arms because the other drivers that were honking at her and pointing out of their windows at her did not get her attention. I finally got her attention and when I did, I told her that her gas mileage was going to be considerably hindered if she continued to pull the blower down the street.

We figured out a couple of things that day. For one thing, the gentleman who volunteered around the building learned where he should not leave his extension cord and electric blower when he went to lunch. We had a funeral for his blower that afternoon. The secretary learned that day how not to use an electric blower. From that day she resolved never to drive over another extension cord.

We laughed that day. No, let me rephrase that, I laughed that day. Anyhow, we may laugh about it, but we have all done some embarrassing things. We have all shared painful moments at times from our own poor choices. All of us have been guilty of demonstrating a lack of good judgment. We all have failed in being prudent, or wise at times in the practical affairs of life. By the time we reach adulthood we learn that in life there are two ways to learn a lesson, the easy way and the hard way.

The sad fact is we are slow learners when it comes to being wise in action. We tend to learn lessons only by the hard way. The easy way for us to acquire wisdom on how to live life comes from listening to what God says. There is hope attached to discovering God's prudence and connecting it to our lives. If we will pay attention to His wisdom, we will be wiser in thought and action.

Proverbs 8:12, *I, wisdom, dwell together with prudence; I possess knowledge and discretion*. True wisdom comes by taking what we learn from God and then applying it to our everyday lives. Paul had prayed for the believers to receive wisdom from above. How do we get this wisdom from above? It comes by hearing or reading what God has revealed to us through the apostles.

The apostle Paul often prayed for our spiritual wisdom and discernment. Ephesians 1:17, *I keep asking that the God of our Lord Jesus Christ, the glorious Father, may give you the Spirit of wisdom and revelation, so that you may know him better.* Colossians 1:9b, *we have not stopped praying for you and asking God to fill you with the knowledge of his will through all spiritual wisdom and understanding.*

The source of spiritual wisdom and understanding comes from God. There is a three-fold formula to gain wisdom. We acquire wisdom by listening to what God says in His Word, obeying it, and actually asking God for wisdom through faithful prayer. That combination sends wisdom our way, and wisdom will help us to live-hope-filled lives. James 1:5, *If any of you lacks wisdom, he should ask God, who gives generously to all without finding fault, and it will be given to him.*

The Bible reveals the information we need to know so we can live as children of light in this dark, sin-filled world. The apostle said in 1 Corinthians 2:6-7, *[6] We do, however, speak a message of wisdom among the mature, but not the wisdom of this age or of the rulers of this age, who are coming to nothing. [7] No, we speak of God's secret wisdom, a wisdom that has been hidden and that God destined for our glory before time began.* God provides us wisdom, and in His wisdom hope, so we can shine into the darkness.

We Christians no longer live in darkness, but there is darkness all around us. Ephesians 5:8-14, *[8] For you were once darkness, but now you are light in the Lord. Live as children of light [9] (for the fruit of the light consists in all goodness, righteousness and truth) [10] and find out what pleases the Lord. [11] Have nothing to do with the fruitless deeds of darkness, but rather expose them. [12] For it is shameful even to mention what the disobedient do in secret. [13] But everything exposed by the light becomes visible, [14] for it is light that makes everything visible. This is why it is said: "Wake up, O sleeper, rise from the dead, and Christ will shine on you."*

We can shine the light of God in the darkness, most brightly by demonstrating godly wisdom. Such wisdom and understanding brings hope and shines light into the darkness. Psalm 119:104-105, *[104] I gain understanding from your precepts; therefore, I hate every wrong path. [105] Your word is a lamp to my feet and a light for my path.* True wisdom shines from a productive prudent life of action. The result of finding hope in God's wisdom enables His light-bearers to be wise in the way they live.

The source of the world's wisdom is the devil and He is the representative of darkness. James 3:14-15, *[14] But if you harbor bitter envy and selfish ambition in your hearts, do not boast about it or deny the truth. [15] Such "wisdom" does not come down from heaven but is earthly, unspiritual, of the devil.* There is an obvious contrast between fruit the children of light produce and the fruit the children of darkness produce. James 3:17, *But the wisdom that comes from heaven is first of all pure; then peace-loving, considerate, submissive, full of mercy and good fruit, impartial and sincere.*

Children of light understand that God's wisdom is wiser than any man's wisdom. 1 Corinthians 1:25, *For the foolishness of God is wiser than man's wisdom, and the weakness of God is stronger than man's strength.* Wise people learn to trust God's prudence while foolish people refuse to acknowledge God's perspective. Psalm 25:4-5, *⁴ Show me your ways, O LORD, teach me your paths; ⁵ guide me in your truth and teach me, for you are God my Savior, and my hope is in you all day long.* God's perspective on how we should live life is always accurate. When we trust God's perspective, we find hope.

My son played on the varsity soccer team all four years in high school. His mother and I watched a lot of soccer games before he entered high school. To those watching a soccer game from the sidelines, when a ball is kicked toward the goal it often looks like the ball is headed straight for the goal – only to go to the left or right, or over the goal. The perspective we get from the sidelines is not accurate. Wisdom is the ability to make good choices which are connected to God's perspective.

Wise people get off the sidelines and live life according to the view God has revealed to them. We must trust God's perspective for He is the only reliable source of wisdom. God's perspective is perfectly accurate and ours, without God's insight, is terribly flawed. Years make us older, but not automatically wiser. But there is great value in attaining wisdom. Ecclesiastes 7:19, *Wisdom makes one wise man more powerful than ten rulers in a city.*

Ecclesiastes 9:17, *The quiet words of the wise are more to be heeded than the shouts of a ruler of fools.* The world does not always acknowledge or appreciate the right things. The world honors power, wealth, and success above God's wisdom. Wisdom is practical and light producing, but it is not appreciated by those who practice disgraceful acts under the cover of darkness (Ephesians 5:12). Wisdom shouts "Wake up!" into the darkness of the spiritually dead.

Ephesians 5:15-17, *15 Be very careful, then, how you live – not as unwise but as wise, 16 making the most of every opportunity, because the days are evil. 17 Therefore do not be foolish, but understand what the Lord's will is.* The English Standard Version reads, *making the best use of the time, because the days are evil* (Ephesians 5:16). The King James Version reads, *Redeeming the time, because the days are evil* (Ephesians 5:16). The Greek word translated "time" or "opportunity" is CARAWAYS. The King James Version and the English Standard Version translates CARAWAYS, "time" in Ephesians 5:16, but in Galatians 6:10, it is translated CARAWAYS, "opportunity." The New International Version uses the word "opportunity" in these two passages.

When we are given time, we are given opportunity. How can we be careful and make the most of our opportunities or make the best use of our time? We are to take advantage of the moments we have been given – time is a gift from God. We have been given time to learn how we should conduct ourselves now so one day we can be with God in the place where time has no value. Here and now we say, "time is money;" however, without time, there is no value in money. Time is more valuable than money in the here and now.

Some people will likely run out of time before they run out of money. Money cannot buy time, but that is alright because we have been given time now to choose how to live. Children of light choose to live by what God values as important. Hope comes from wise use of the time God has given us, because time is fleeting, eternity is forever. We must use our time wisely and we use it wisely by understanding the Lord's will (Ephesians 5:17).

According to Ecclesiastes 3:1-8, there is time for everything. Ecclesiastes 3:1-2, *¹ There is a time for everything, and a season for every activity under heaven: ² a time to be born and a time to die, a time to plant and a time to uproot.* Solomon shared a list of fourteen pairs of things over which we have little to no control over, but there is a time for everything. I have noticed some people are better than others at managing their time. Being able to manage our time has nothing to do with having more time than others.

I realized years ago that if something really needed to get done around the church building or in the ministry, it was advantageous to ask someone who was already busy to do it. Of course, it is also beneficial to ask someone who is not busy to step up and do something. This can promote and encourage personal growth in their work in the Lord's kingdom. However, my point of asking someone busy when we have something that really needs to get done, is they will find the time to do it. Why? Because they are often the people who are making the best use of time.

Using our time wisely has a lot to do with how we view eternity. I knew a fellow who was late all the time. If he had an appointment– he was late. Everyone was aware of his problem of being late. One day the man came to my office to visit with me about his problem of time management. He confessed what I already knew about his struggle with coordinating his time. He spoke of his frustration with always being late.

The fellow's tardiness had an impact on everything he did. He was late to really important things and late to things that were not as important. So, being the highly trained, wise preacher that I am, I asked him. "Do you own a watch?" He said, "No, I have never worn a watch – it bothers me to wear a watch." Not wearing a watch was not the cause of his problem; but wearing one probably would have helped him correct the problem.

I have found for myself I have a lot better chance to make the most of my time when I am aware of the time. In our day most people who do not wear a watch are carrying around a cell phone with the time on the home screen. I like to know the approximate time because it helps me to manage my time. But whether we wear a watch or not, we all live in a world that is either going to use its time wisely or foolishly. To use our time wisely we need to put the concept of time in the context of our ultimate destination.

Time is temporary, but time allows us to understand that the Lord's goal for us is eternity with Him. A person may never be late for an appointment and manage his time well. But we should not be deceived in thinking because we are rarely late that we are managing our time in accordance with the Lord's will. Ephesians 5 speaks to using our time of opportunity wisely. We cannot do that without realigning our values to God's values.

Let us not be foolish with the time and opportunities God has given us. Let us be careful to be diverted from living as children of light. We cannot walk appropriately without understanding the Lord's will. Therefore, we must learn what pleases God, and this requires us to get into the Word of God. Reading the Bible helps us to put wisdom to work in our lives. Wisdom does work. God's wisdom works hope in us.

There is great benefit to being careful specifically in how we live. Proverbs 14:15, *A simple man believes anything, but a prudent man gives thought to his steps.* The words "prudent" or "prudence" are found collectively around fifteen times in Proverbs. There are great benefits to living wisely. Proverbs 2:9-12, *⁹ Then you will understand what is right and just and fair – every good path. ¹⁰ For wisdom will enter your heart, and knowledge will be pleasant to your soul. ¹¹ Discretion will protect you, and understanding will guard you. ¹² Wisdom will save you from the ways of wicked men, from men whose words are perverse.*

Wisdom helps to have the right view – God's view. *If you are wise, your wisdom will reward you* (Proverbs 9:12a). We must be careful how we walk and live because evil is at work. There are evil influences at work in the world. If we are not prudent, we will not be the lights God expects us to be in this world of darkness. If we do not pay careful attention to how we live, we will lose the opportunity to fulfill God's purpose as His lights.

We do not have to learn every valuable lesson the hard way if we will commit ourselves to understanding the Lord's will. Spirit-filled people are hope-filled people. Hope-filled living is Spirit-filled living. Ephesians 5:18, *Do not get drunk on wine,*

which leads to debauchery. Instead, be filled with the Spirit.
Drunkenness is of the darkness and leads to all sorts of other
evil things. Spirit-filled living will keep us away from being
deceived by the Deceiver. Proverbs 20:1, *Wine is a mocker and
beer a brawler; whoever is led astray by them is not wise.* The
English Standard Version reads in Proverbs 20:1, *Wine is a
mocker, strong drink a brawler, and whoever is led astray by it
is not wise.*

Spirit-filled living is living wisely. It is further summed up in
Ephesians 5:19-20, *[19] Speak to one another with psalms, hymns
and spiritual songs. Sing and make music in your heart to the
Lord, [20] always giving thanks to God the Father for everything,
in the name of our Lord Jesus Christ.* How we speak and
interact with each other and to God the Father and the Lord
Jesus Christ is crucial to our spiritual health. Spirit-filled people
will express uplifting and encouraging words in a world that
commonly tears down and spits out discouraging words.

The lights from thankful people glow brightly as they ring out
the eternal melody of hope they have in their hearts to the
Lord. We can make a difference in the world for God as we are
filled with the Spirit. Spirit-filled people follow the prudent
teaching handed down to them in Ephesians 5:8-20. Spirit-filled
living understands it is the Lord's will that His children always
be a thankful people. Thankful people express their gratitude
to God by being careful about what they say and how they live.

Godly wisdom is reflected by the light we shine in our
relationships and interactions with people. Jesus spoke of His
people being *the light of the world* (Matthew 5:14). In
Matthew 5:16, Jesus said, *In the same way, let your light shine*

before men, that they may see your good deeds and praise your Father in heaven. The light of the Lord provides both direction and deliverance. Therefore, the light of Christians beams out into the darkness giving hope to those who will seek God. There is great hope attached to living in the light of the Lord's wisdom.

CHAPTER 11 – QUESTIONS
TO DISCUSS, DEVELOP, AND DETERMINE

1. What did the Apostle Paul often ask for in his prayers for Christians?

2. What is a three-fold formula for acquiring wisdom in our lives?

3. God's perspective on how we should live life is always accurate. What do we find when we trust God's perspective?

4. How can we shine the light of God most brightly in our lives?

5. How can we make the most of our opportunities and the best use of our time? What do we need to realign to use out time wisely?

6. What did Solomon say in regarding time? What does that tell us?

7. Using our time wisely has a lot to do with our having a certain view. What is that view?

8. What are some traits of Spirit-filled people? Hope-filled living is what kind of living according to Ephesians 5:18?

Chapter 12

FIND HOPE IN GOD'S PLAN
(Ephesians 5:21-6:9)

There is a hope for those who will follow God's blueprint for marriage. God has a plan for those who choose to marry, have a family, and for all employers and employees in the workplace. Let us begin with God's successful plan for those who enter the covenant relationship of marriage. Since God designed marriage it is beneficial to follow His plan. When we follow God's strategy for having a successful marriage, we will find hope in God's plan.

I recently conducted a wedding ceremony for a couple. As I write this chapter our country is under siege with the virus called Coved-19. The couple asked me to do their ceremony prior to our being mandated to practice social distancing. It was not ever going to be a big wedding, but after the guidelines to slow the curve of the virus came down from the President, the Governor, and the local officials, they asked me if I would still do the ceremony if it was just them. I said, "I will if we will apply the social distancing guidelines."

The couple wanted to be married outside on top of a small mountain. I met them there and they were married. Their love for each other had led them to want to make a lifelong commitment and that afternoon with the wind blowing and my standing several feet away, they were joined in marriage. I reminded them their love would need to continue to be shaped by God's love and God's plan for a heavenly marriage.

If newlyweds will value what God values, they will find hope in God's plan for marriage. Value refers to worth. Values will direct our thoughts, attitudes, and decisions. We need to know what God values because it is those values that should determine our behavior. My wife Lori and I rarely go grocery shopping together. Here is why we tend to go shopping without each other. My wife sees an item and she will pick it up and put it in the cart and never looks at the price. Now that is the way many people shop. There is nothing wrong with that approach, but it is not my approach and I have had to learn to adapt to her shopping approach.

The way I shop for groceries is much different, and a lot of people shop the way I do. I want to compare every item to the other similar items on the nearby shelf. I will always look at the price tag before I put anything in my cart. Now I compare items and look at the price not simply because I am looking for the least expensive item but I want to know the price before I get to the checkout line. For example, I may choose to buy the most expensive peanut butter on the shelf because I like the taste, but I know the price of the item before I get in the checkout line.

In fact, I nearly refuse to put something in my cart without a price on it. I think other people ought to thank me for this. How many times have we been in the line at the grocery store and the person in front of us has an item with no price on it? What do they have to do? They have to wait for someone to get a price check. They wait and we wait behind them in the checkout line simply because the individual picked up the one item that was missing a sticker.

Perhaps my time of working in a grocery store when I was in high school contributes to my making sure there is a price tag on the item. Anyhow it did not take long after we were married to know we shop differently, and that is alright. But as a husband I had to take God's Word through Peter and apply them to my marriage. God's teaching on how to have a successful marriage depends to some degree on my desire to live with my wife in a considerate and understanding way.

We must not let our differences of opinion disrupt God's beautiful plan for marriage. 1 Peter 3:7, *Husbands, in the same way be considerate as you live with your wives, and treat them with respect as the weaker partner and as heirs with you of the gracious gift of life, so that nothing will hinder your prayers.* The word "partner" in verse 7, is not found in the original language. The original Greek reveals the term "weaker vase" or "weaker vessel."

The English Standard Version reads, *Likewise, husbands, live with your wives in an understanding way, showing honor to the woman as the weaker vessel, since they are heirs with you of the grace of life, so that your prayers may not be hindered* (1 Peter 3:7). The idea behind the phrase "an understanding way," or "be considerate," literally means "according to knowledge." The husband is to learn how to treat his wife according to God's knowledge of His word and her physical, emotional, and spiritual needs.

The "weaker vessel" phrase in the English Standard Version or the term "weaker partner" in the New International Version points out that the wife is to be treated with special care. The weaker literal vessels we might have in our homes are the most valuable vessels. The husband is to treat his wife as a delicate, valuable piece of china or crystal in comparison to a common inexpensive clay vessel. The metal vase may be much stronger, but much less valuable. The wife is to be treated as a special, made-in-the-image of God woman. She is to be treated with the utmost value and respect.

The word "honor" or "heirs" in 1 Peter 3:7, gives more insight on how a husband is to treat his wife. He is to treat her with dignity and esteem her. Husbands are responsible for cherishing their wives in the grace of life. Husbands and wives can see things differently, show grace, and be loving to one another. The marriage that will blossom into a hope-filled marriage is one where both the husband and the wife will see how God values them and practice God's values on each other.

It is worth noting the first six verses prior to 1 Peter 3:7 addresses women who became Christians after they were married and now find themselves married to an unbeliever. It would be difficult for such a spouse to follow God's plan, but they needed to know God has a plan in such a situation. If the Christian will follow God's plan, it will be evidence they recognize what God's values.

1 Peter 3:1-6, [1] *Wives, in the same way be submissive to your husbands so that, if any of them do not believe the word, they may be won over without words by the behavior of their wives,* [2] *when they see the purity and reverence of your lives.* [3] *Your beauty should not come from outward adornment, such as braided hair and the wearing of gold jewelry and fine clothes.* [4] *Instead, it should be that of your inner self, the unfading beauty of a gentle and quiet spirit, which is of great worth in*

God's sight. ⁵ For this is the way the holy women of the past who put their hope in God used to make themselves beautiful. They were submissive to their own husbands, ⁶ like Sarah, who obeyed Abraham and called him her master. You are her daughters if you do what is right and do not give way to fear.

We will discuss the value of submission in detail shortly, but for now it will be helpful to get a grasp on the context of 1 Peter 3:7. It better helps us understand how a Christian husband is to live with his wife. The New International Version reads, *Husbands, in the same way be considerate as you live with your wives, and treat them with respect as the weaker partner and as heirs with you of the gracious gift of life, so that nothing will hinder your prayers* (1 Peter 3:7). Obviously, it is vitally important we husbands get this down right or our prayers will not reach beyond the ceiling.

1 Peter 3:1 begins with the words, "in the same way" or "likewise." What is Peter getting at here? To understand we should note Chapter 2 ends by mentioning the attitude and example of Jesus in a difficult circumstance. Therefore, the words "likewise" or "in the same way," refers to how Jesus was the absolute great example of submission. Submission is not so much about trusting our spouses as it is about trusting God.

Submission is a sign that a person values what God values (Ephesians 5:21). God's plan requires we value what God values. We must value God's understanding of submission and love to have a heavenly marriage. It takes two to have a great marriage, but one who will follow God's plan will make a marriage considerably better. God gives us some of His strategy for a Christian marriage in Ephesians 5:21-33.

Ephesians 5:21-33, *²¹ Submit to one another out of reverence for Christ. ²² Wives, submit to your husbands as to the Lord. ²³ For the husband is the head of the wife as Christ is the head of the church, his body, of which he is the Savior. ²⁴ Now as the church submits to Christ, so also wives should submit to their husbands in everything. ²⁵ Husbands, love your wives, just as Christ loved the church and gave himself up for her ²⁶ to make her holy, cleansing her by the washing with water through the word, ²⁷ and to present her to himself as a radiant church, without stain or wrinkle or any other blemish, but holy and blameless. ²⁸ In this same way, husbands, ought to love their wives as their own bodies. He who loves his wife loves himself. ²⁹ After all, no one ever hated his own body, but he feeds and cares for it, just as Christ does the church – ³⁰ for we are members of his body. ³¹ "For this reason a man will leave his father and mother and be united to his wife, and the two will become one flesh." ³² This is a profound mystery – but I am talking about Christ and the church. ³³ However, each one of you also must love his wife as he loves himself, and the wife must respect her husband.*

The truths found here are universal principles that will work if we put them into practice whether we have been married for five days, five months, or fifty years. The more we apply them, the greater and more fulfilling our marriage can become. If we ignore God's blueprint for marriage, our marriage will deteriorate. The husband is called to love his wife in a sacrificial way.

We learn in Ephesians 5:21 that submission for the husband and the wife is not a bad word. If a wife struggles in the area of submission, she should remember that because Jesus submitted to the Father did not mean He was inferior in any way to the Father. If a wife struggles in the area of submission, the husband should check his own definition of love. Husbands need to make sure their definition of love is in line with God's definition found in 1 Corinthians 13.

1 Corinthians 13:4-7, [4] *Love is patient, love is kind. It does not envy, it does not boast, it is not proud.* [5] *It is not rude, it is not self-seeking, it is not easily angered, it keeps no record of wrongs.* [6] *Love does not delight in evil but rejoices with the truth.* [7] *It always protects, always trusts, always hopes, always perseveres.* It is our actions, not our words, that demonstrate God's kind of love in a marriage.

A husband is not going to be perfect in loving his wife, but he needs to be committed to trying to be perfectly loving and submissive. In the same way, a wife is not going to be perfect in loving her husband, but she needs to be committed to trying to be perfectly loving and submissive.

I have had more than a few husbands come to me over the years and tell me I needed to tell their wife to submit to them. Something is quite wrong with that picture! Every time a husband has done that, I have found major spiritual problems occurring in the life of the man. The husband who has abused the word submission and has made the concept to mean anything he wants has created serious roadblocks in his marriage. Ephesians 5:23, "*For the husband is head of the wife,*" and the term "head" in the original refers to a person leading another for the sake of their highest good.

The husband is to spiritually lead his wife for her highest good as he follows God's plan for loving His wife. When a wife submits to her husband it does not mean she is inferior to her husband in any way, but rather she has chosen to follow God's plan for marriage. Understood correctly submission is a freedom word that brings a wife to a deeper level of intimacy with the Lord and greater influence in her marriage. The word submission has been abused, misused, and misunderstood by both men and women, but submission is part of God's plan for marriage.

There is also hope to be found from following God's blueprint for the family. Ephesians 6:1-4, *[1] Children, obey your parents in the Lord, for this is right. [2] "Honor your father and mother" – which is the first commandment with a promise – [3] "that it may go well with you and that you may enjoy long life on the earth." [4] Fathers, do not exasperate your children; instead, bring them up in the training and instruction of the Lord.*

God lays down here a clear and direct charge to children which will contribute to having a great family. Imagine what it must have been like to be sitting in the general assembly and hearing the Ephesian letter read for the first time. How exciting it must have been to hear again the story of Jesus' love. The story about a love so high, deep, wide and long it moves us. Imagine eagerly listening to the latest Word from God and the reader comes to Ephesians 6:1, and says "children."

After hearing the word children, we would expect the children's ears to perk up and their eyes to light up and be tuned to hear what words will be said. We cannot know what they might expect to hear. Perhaps they were anticipating more words about Jesus sacrifice. Maybe they were expecting the words of inspiration to say something like, "Jesus loves all the children," and of course Jesus loves children. But instead of hearing, "Jesus Loves Me," the words that follow the word "children" is a call to obey their parents in the Lord.

Children still need to hear this message. The word "obey" means to listen thoughtfully. Obedience requires thoughtfulness and movement. Walk into any store and there is a decent chance we will find a child being disrespectful to a parent. Children will be children, but parents that allow their child to continue to be disrespectful are not helping their child. In this case, we have a child and a parent not following God's plan for the family.

Hope is available for families who will follow God's plan. The child who has no respect for parental authority will have no respect for the greatest authority in the universe, which is God. The phrase connected to a child obeying their parents is an important one. The phrase, "In the Lord," means in harmony with the Lord's teaching. Children cannot be rebellious with their parents and be right with the Lord. Children also need to practice submission to their parents out of reverence for Christ.

The father is the one that needs to take the lead his family in loving the Lord, serving the Lord, and obeying the Lord. It is a choice we have to make and our choice will affect the measure of hope we have and ultimately where we will spend eternity. Ephesians 6:4, *Fathers, do not exasperate your children; instead, bring them up in the training and instruction of the Lord.* The English Standard Version reads, *Fathers, do not provoke your children to anger, but bring them up in the discipline and instruction of the Lord* (Ephesians 6:4).

Fathers and all Christian parents are to be spiritual mentors in developing good and godly attitudes in their children. Christian parents are to bring their children up in the Lord. Fathers are given the primary responsibility of being the spiritual coach in the family. The word "training" in the New International Version carries the idea of coaching with instruction. Spiritual coaching gives spiritual direction.

A father that follow God's plan for the family is a hope-filled father. A spiritual father is the coach that leads by example. The godly father's example in the home can make a wonderful difference in the lives of those who reside in the family. Fathers and mothers share in the responsibility of bringing up their children in the Lord. But in Ephesians 6:4, God gives precise instruction to fathers.

Father are not to "exasperate" or "provoke" their children. Fathers are prone to just that so we have a similar teaching in Colossians. Colossians 3:21, *Fathers, do not embitter your children, or they will become discouraged*. This is God's charge to fathers. Raising children is a blessing, but it is work. I heard someone say, "Raising children can be like nailing Jell-O to a tree." Parenting can be difficult, but it is also a great blessing, and children are gifts from God.

As fathers we should not expect our children to do what they are unable to do. Our expectations must be reasonable and in line with their age and maturity. We can frustrate and discourage by putting more on them then they are capable of handling. Fathers must not load their children down with burdens they cannot bear. On the other hand, we should expect what we know they are capable of doing, even if their capabilities are limited.

Fathers and mothers need to remember God is never unreasonable with us. God never puts more on us then we can bear. Therefore, we should not have unreasonable expectations from our children. Let us remember that encouragement goes a long way in nurturing our children. Everyone responds better to improvement when we are encouraged for doing well. Parents share the responsibility to place before their children the attitudes of Jesus.

The Christian father leads with a purpose. He leads with the same desire that motivated Paul to do ministry. Galatians 4:19, *My dear children, for whom I am again in the pains of childbirth until Christ is formed in you.* By our pointing out the value of good attitudes versus bad attitudes, our children learn what God values. When they understand God's values and align God's values in what they value, they will find a hope that is not of this world.

There is hope to be found as well from following God's blueprint for employees and employers. Ephesians 6:5-9, [5] *Slaves, obey your earthly masters with respect and fear, and with sincerity of heart, just as you would obey Christ.* [6] *Obey them not only to win their favor when their eye is on you, but like slaves of Christ, doing the will of God from your heart.* [7] *Serve wholeheartedly, as if you were serving the Lord, not men,* [8] *because you know that the Lord will reward everyone for whatever good he does, whether he is slave or free.* [9] *And masters, treat your slaves in the same way. Do not threaten them, since you know that he who is both their Master and yours is in heaven, and there is no favoritism with him.*

In the first century Roman world, slaves were plentiful. They had slaves who served in homes, in the fields, and in every kind of job we could imagine. Some slaves were treated well and were respected and appreciated by their masters. Other slaves were led by uncaring and mean-spirited masters. In either case, Christian slaves and masters in the first century were given God's plan on how to conduct themselves.

Masters who became Christians would want their slaves to become Christians. Slaves who had become Christians prayed their masters would also follow Christ's teaching. It is understandable that in a world that was practicing slavery at differing levels, God gave a guideline for masters and slaves to follow. God's plan involved obedience to the masters and respect and hard work from the slaves. God also expected those responsible for slaves to be just and fair.

Colossians 3:22, *Slaves, obey your earthly masters in everything; and do it, not only when their eye is on you and to win their favor, but with sincerity of heart and reverence for the Lord.* Colossians 4:1, *Masters, provide your slaves with what is right and fair, because you know that you also have a Master in heaven.* Christian masters and slaves needed to show respect for each other, for they were following the same Master, the Lord Jesus the Christ.

Today, we can readily apply the teaching to how Christian employers and employees are to conduct themselves in the workplace. The Christian employer was to serve the Lord and treat people without favoritism. Employees were to serve the Lord by serving their masters well. Some masters were cruel, harshly demanding, and threatening to their slaves. The master or supervisor who became a Christian and had previously been threatening his slaves needed to stop threatening them.

The guiding principle of value God gives us in this section is to treat people as we would want them to treat us. There are unbelieving employers today that are similarly condescending and harsh to their Christian employees. In such a case, the Christian is to serve their employer well, just as if they were serving the Lord, not men. This section is about treating people right whether we are in authority over someone or under someone else's authority. The apostle reminds both employer and employee that they stand together under the authority of Christ.

Colossians 3:23, *Whatever you do, work at it with all your heart, as working for the Lord, not for men*. The Christian worker shows the sincerity of his faith by serving wholeheartedly his employer, whether he his kind and understanding, or mean and inconsiderate. Ephesians 3:8 tells us the good we do will not go unnoticed by God. God will reward us for following His plan in the workplace. By following God's plan in marriage, in the family, and in the workplace, we find hope.

CHAPTER 12 – QUESTIONS
TO DISCUSS, DEVELOP, AND DETERMINE

1. What would a married couple need to find hope in God's plan for marriage? What impact should this understanding have on our behavior? Marriage blossoms into a hope-filled marriage when a couple will do what?

2. What does the idea behind the phrase "an understanding way," or "be considerate," literally mean? Explain how a husband can live with his wife in an understanding way.

3. What does the phrase "weaker vessel" in the English Standard Version mean?

4. Understood correctly "submission" is what kind of word? How have some men contributed to some women having the idea that submission is a bad word? Explain what sign can we take away from a man or a woman submitting to one another out of reverence for Christ.

5. What does it mean for children to obey their parents in the Lord?

6. What primary responsibility is a father given with his children? What is a father to be careful not to do in Ephesians 6:4 and Colossians 3:21? Explain how a father can avoid doing do this.

7. Why did Christian masters or slaves in the first century need to show respect for each other?

8. What is the guiding principle of value that we can take away from Ephesians 6:5-9?

FIND HOPE IN GOD'S PROTECTION
(Ephesians 6:10-17, 21-24)

There is a battle cry that rings out to all the Christians in Ephesians 6:10, *Finally be strong in the Lord and in His mighty power.* After we confess our sins and are truly sorry for them and obey the gospel, God lifts us up out of the pit of sin, we have buried ourselves in and forgives us. At which time, *God raised us up with Christ and seated us with him in the heavenly realms in Christ Jesus* (Ephesians 2:6). After we are saved by grace we must continue to lean on God's protective power because Satan does not stop coming after us.

Ephesians 6:11-12, *[11] Put on the full armor of God so that you can take your stand against the devil's schemes. [12] For our struggle is not against flesh and blood, but against the rulers, against the authorities, against the powers of this dark world and against the spiritual forces of evil in the heavenly realms.* We are in a conflict with the spiritual forces of evil that we cannot avoid. We must prepare for battle God's way.

We need to practice spiritual discernment and be alert to Satan's deceptions. Psalm 31:24, *Be strong and take heart, all you who hope in the LORD.* A few years ago, I had scheduled a fishing trip on the Colorado River. My friend and I joined a fishing guide who used oars to guide us about eight miles downstream in his small boat. As we floated down the river, my friend used a spinning rod to fish while I chose a fly rod to cast towards the river bank.

It was a beautiful sunny day with a little breeze off the water, making the temperature comfortable. It was so beautiful I would not have cared if I even caught a fish that day. But I did catch several and one of the biggest bass I had ever caught fly fishing. The fish weighed nearly five pounds and I took a picture of it to prove it, since I returned it to the water. As we were enjoying the rejuvenating experience that day, we had little concern about anything else. My only issue was trying not to get my fishing line hung up in the big oak tree limbs that hovered over the water.

My primary and only concern that morning as I began fishing was not to tangle my line in the trees because the current of the water was steadily moving the boat down steam. If I did get my line snagged, it would likely break my line and I would lose my lure. It was not long after we started our trip that I added another concern, which not only added to my main concern, it became my main concern.

The fishing guide pointed up into a tree and asked if we could see the water moccasin (Cottonmouth) camouflaged on a tree limb. It took me a moment to actually see it. We had almost passed by it before I could distinguish the snake from the limb. He told us that the moccasins had fallen into his boat on several occasions.

The snakes climb up on the trees to get a better view of any fish in the water passing under the trees. We were surprised to learn that he had experienced these types of snakes actually drop from the trees into his boat when they saw his catch of fish. Therefore, he warned us to be on our watch for these snakes. We heeded his advice and appreciated it.

Water moccasins are deceitful. They are masters at camouflaging themselves and their schemes of catching their prey are deceptive. These snakes are aggressive and their venom toxic. We were on the lookout for them during our fishing trip. Christians are warned about the devil's schemes and we are told we need to be on high alert.

We are promised victory over Satan, but the victory comes by putting on God's protective armor. We can move forward with God's armor in place and find hope in the protection He provides us. Victory in Christ is possible when we resolve to be strong in the Lord. We cannot do battle with Satan on our own power or we will face spiritual disaster.

The battle we fight is sandwiched between light and darkness, good and bad, and heaven and hell. We cannot run from this battle and know victory. We cannot hide from this battle and be victors. We need to stand in the strength of the Lord and move forward in His power. Let us remember that when we attempt to battle the spiritual forces of evil with our own strength, we will be defeated.

We find in the final chapter of Ephesians a military metaphor. We have a metaphor about putting on the armor of God, and this armor coincided with the armor worn by Roman soldiers. We live out our Christian lives on the battlefield. We are in a battle against enemies we cannot always see.

Ephesians 6:13-17, [13] *Therefore put on the full armor of God, so that when the day of evil comes, you may be able to stand your ground, and after you have done everything, to stand.* [14] *Stand firm then, with the belt of truth buckled around your waist, with the breastplate of righteousness in place, [15] and with your feet fitted with the readiness that comes from the gospel of peace. [16] In addition to all this, take up the shield of faith, with which you can extinguish all the flaming arrows of the evil one. [17] Take the helmet of salvation and the sword of the Spirit, which is the word of God.*

The description of the armor begins with the belt of truth. The soldier's belt was used to tie up anything that might hinder a soldier. It was buckled down around the waist and brought support around the middle of the body. The belt of truth buckled around our waist implies battle readiness. We must commit ourselves to following the truth of God.

We will never accomplish much in the kingdom of God if our lives are not based on truth. We can only take our stand successfully against Satan when we stand on the fact that Jesus is the TRUTH. Truth is personified in the person of Jesus. Therefore, we need to tuck our doubts into God's belt of truth so we can avoid being deceived by Satan's schemes.

The breastplate of the Roman soldier covered the chest for protection to vital organs. These breastplates were custom molded by a skilled craftsman employed by the Roman government to personally fit soldiers. The soldier did not have anything to do with making them. In the same way we are fitted with the breastplate of righteousness. We do not make it, earn it, but we are to wear the breastplate of righteousness.

The righteousness we wear places us on the road to standing firm against the enemy. When we obey the gospel, we are covered by the righteousness of Jesus (2 Corinthians 5:21). As

Jesus was dying on the cross, He molded His righteousness that would cover and protect all those who would trust in His righteousness.

Another part of a soldier's armor is *feet fitted with the readiness that comes from the gospel of peace*. We are talking about wearing shoes appropriate for battle. Most of us have several kinds of shoes at home. I have what I call Sunday shoes, kickaround sandals, lawn mowing shoes, and water repellent fishing shoes. I use these shoes for a variety of different purposes.

The Roman soldier equipped for battle wore a shoe that had spikes driven down through the soles. They were basically like cleats that some athletes wear in competition. Any soldier that could stand firm would be at an advantage in battle. When we wear the gospel of peace as cleats on our feet, we can stand secure no matter the landscape.

Having our shoes fitted with the gospel of peace means we will keep standing upright when Satan launches his evil attacks. It is worth noting the word "stand" is found four times in Ephesians 6:11-14. The gospel is the good news that stabilizes us and gives us leverage to stand strong in battle. The gospel of peace gives us an inner peace because we know we have eternal life.

Faith is our shield against the evil one. Faith makes the difference between victory and defeat. Ephesians 6:16, *In addition to all this, take up the shield of faith, with which you can extinguish all the flaming arrows of the evil one.* The Christian shield is connected by the word "faith" and of course it is the faith which is rooted in Jesus that shields and protects us. We have hope when we are under the Devil's attacks. Psalm 33:20, *We wait in hope for the LORD; he is our help and our shield.*

When the flaming arrows are shot in our direction as soldiers of Christ, we can take up the shield of faith and find protection by faith in God's truth. When Satan projects into our minds the flaming arrows to get us to doubt God, we need to take up the shield of faith. There were two types of shields carried by Roman soldiers. One was a small, lightweight round shield. He would strap it to his arm and use it to protect himself against knife cuts and blows in little skirmishes around the city. The second type of shield was approximately 2½ feet wide, and about 4½ feet tall.

The shield under discussion in Ephesians 6:16 was the larger shield. It was more of a full-body battle shield that soldiers used to protect their body. This shield was made of metal and often covered with a layer of leather that could be drenched in water. Flaming arrows were a dreaded weapon. The arrows had strips of cloth wrapped around them that could be lit prior to being shot. The particular shield Paul speaks of and applies to the Christian armor represented protection from flaming arrows. The metal would stop the arrows while the soaked leather could extinguish them.

There was another unique feature to some of these larger Roman shields. Soldiers could use them individually, but they also could be joined with another soldier's shield. This would allow them to more readily withstand the onslaught of flaming arrows. This shield was a great help in Rome's many victories. When an enemy no longer had any more arrows, the soldiers could advance and win. Christians are to take up their spiritual shields and unite against the enemy.

Another key to experiencing spiritual victory is putting on the helmet of salvation. Ephesians 6:17, *Take the helmet of salvation and the sword of the Spirit, which is the word of God.* The helmet in the Christian armor is one of the most important pieces. It is one thing to get a blow to the body and it is quite a different matter to get a blow to the head. The head must be protected from injury. This is why bicycle riders wear helmets and construction crews wear hard-hats. Football players know how important it is to wear their helmets on the field. The football helmet is designed by the engineers to pad the head from a hard hit or blow as well as to protect the head from serious damage.

It would be terrible to break an arm or a leg, but we understand an injury to the head is often fatal. Soldiers in the Roman army wore helmets because they knew the value of having their head protected in battle. Christians are told to put on the helmet God provides for our protection. Paul identifies our protective helmet to our salvation. The word "salvation" would serve the Christian soldier as protection and give him hope by bringing salvation assurance into the battle.

There is second part of the armor that Paul mentions in Ephesians 6:17 that he refers to as *the sword of the Spirit.* What is this sword? Paul goes on to explain that this sword *is the word of God.* The sword of the Spirit is the Word of God given to us by the Holy Spirit. The sword of the Spirit can be used offensively and defensively.

Jesus used the Scripture offensively and defensively in Matthew 4. Three times Jesus defended Himself with passages of Scripture against Satan's assaults. The third time after defending Himself He went on the offense. Matthew 4:10-11, *[10] Jesus said to him, "Away from me, Satan! For it is written: 'Worship the Lord your God, and serve him only.'" [11] Then the devil left him, and angels came and attended him.* We realize it was only a temporary departure, but the point is that Satan was not going to hang around for long with the sword of God being used against him.

Jesus is the truth we wear around our waist. He is the righteousness we wear as a breastplate. He is the gospel of peace that anchors our feet to stand against the enemy. He is the object of our faith that shields us and keeps us spiritually safe before the enemy. Jesus is our assurance of salvation we wear as a helmet as we take up the sword of the Spirit and use the Word on battlefield of life.

The only way we can stand firm as a solider at war, even when we are wearing the armor of God, is by bowing our hearts in prayer. We addressed prayer from Ephesians 6:18, back in chapter three as we discussed God's praying people. However, we ought to see that prayer is a vital part of the armor God wants us to use that helps to spiritually protect us.

This command to pray is found alongside the description of a Christian's armor and spiritual warfare. Ephesians 6:18, *And pray in the Spirit on all occasions with all kinds of prayers and requests. With this in mind, be alert and always keep on praying for all the saints.* We are to pray continually, personally, and specifically for each other. Prayer is the lifeline and strength of a soldier fighting against the forces of evil in this dark world.

Paul mentioned one of God's loyal soldiers as he closed out Ephesians. Ephesians 6:21-22, *[21] Tychicus, the dear brother and faithful servant in the Lord, will tell you everything, so that you also may know how I am and what I am doing. [22] I am sending him to you for this very purpose, that you may know how we are, and that he may encourage you.* Tychicus was a loyal servant of the Lord and a loyal friend to Paul who helped him with missionary and evangelistic efforts. Paul called him a *"dear brother and faithful servant."*

Paul spoke favorably of Tychicus in Colossians 4:7b. He called him *a faithful minister and fellow servant in the Lord.* He was a spiritual friend to Paul and he shared with Paul in the hope of Christ. Their hope enabled them to help others find strength in God. Tychicus was a true spiritual friend who willing sacrificed for the sake of the kingdom. Christians fight the good fight together as God provides us protection by His abounding grace.

Paul opened his letter by offering the grace and peace of Jesus to these Christians and grace and peace comes up again at the close of his letter. Ephesians 6:23-24, *[23] Peace to the brothers, and love with faith from God the Father and the Lord Jesus Christ. [24] Grace to all who love our Lord Jesus Christ with an undying love.* Peace, love, faith, and grace make a wonderful quartet, but let us not forget about the inspiring word hope. A friend of mine asked me a question when I told him about my desire to write a book on hope. The question was thought provoking. When he told me the answer, I knew it would likely show up in my book; I just did not think it would be in the final paragraph.

My friend's question went something like this: What one word would I use to describe the difference between a Christian and a non-Christian? He gave me several words to think about. Would it be the word, helpful? Would it be the word, goodness? Perhaps it would be the word purity or righteousness. All those words could be used and have been used to describe a Christian. However, the word he used to describe the difference between a Christian and a non-Christian was the word hope. Hope is the most beautiful word for us who believe.

CHAPTER 13 – QUESTIONS
TO DISCUSS, DEVELOP, AND DETERMINE

1. What does not stop after we become Christians? What do we need to do about it?

2. What are Christian warned about in Ephesians 6:11?

3. In practical terms what does the belt of truth imply? What does this piece of the Christian armor help us to avoid?

4. What action did Jesus take that allows us to put on the breastplate of righteousness?

5. Explain how having our shoes fitted with the gospel of peace helps us in our battle against our spiritual enemy. What does the gospel of peace mean in practical terms?

6. Explain the value of taking up the shield of faith and what it helps us to do.

7. How does the helmet of salvation help us? How does our having salvation protect us and bring us hope?

8. What is the sword of the Spirit? How can it be used against Satan's assaults? What word might best describe the difference between a Christian and a non-Christian?

Printed in the USA
CPSIA information can be obtained
at www.ICGtesting.com
JSHW012115171223
53895JS00013B/424